PASS Cambridge BEC Vantage

Second Edition

Workbook with Answer Key

Ian Wood

T0349560

PASS
Cambridge
BEC Vantage

Second Edition

Workbook with Answer Key

Ian Wood

Australia • Brazil • Japan • Korea • Mexico • Singapore • Spain • United Kingdom • United States

Pass Cambridge BEC Vantage Workbook, Second Edition
Ian Wood

Publisher: Jason Mann

Senior Commissioning Editor: John Waterman

Editorial Project Manager: Karen White

Development Editor: Heidi North

Content Project Editor: Denise Power

Production Controller: Tom Relf

Marketing and Communications Manager:
 Michelle Cresswell

Head of Production and Manufacturing:
 Alissa McWhinnie

Compositor: MPS Limited, a Macmillan Company

Text Design: InPraxis

Cover Design: Maria Papageorgiou

ISBN-13: 978-1-133-31655-8

National Geographic Learning
Cheriton House, North Way, Andover, Hampshire, SP10 5BE
United Kingdom

Cengage Learning is a leading provider of customised learning solutions with office locations around the globe, including Singapore, the United Kingdom, Australia, Mexico, Brazil and Japan. Locate our local office at **international.cengage.com/region**

Cengage Learning products are represented in Canada by Nelson Education Ltd.

Visit National Geographic Learning online at **ngl.cengage.com**

Visit our corporate website at **www.cengage.com**

Printed in the United Kingdom by Ashford Colour Press Ltd.
Print Number: 09   Print Year: 2022

Introduction

The Cambridge Business English Certificate

The Cambridge Business English Certificate (BEC) is an international Business English examination which offers a language qualification for learners who use, or will need to use, English for their work. It is available at three levels.

Level 1 Preliminary
Level 2 Vantage
Level 3 Higher

Cambridge BEC is a practical examination that focuses on English in business-related situations. The emphasis is on the development of language skills for work: reading, writing, listening and speaking.

Pass Cambridge BEC Vantage

As an examination preparation course, *Pass Cambridge BEC Vantage* focuses on all the language skills tested at BEC Vantage (reading, writing, listening and speaking) as well as the examination skills required to fully prepare students who wish to take the exam.

Pass Cambridge BEC Vantage Workbook

As an important component of the *Pass Cambridge BEC Vantage* course, the Workbook is a language-focused supplement to the Student's book. Each four-page unit is split into a grammar and a vocabulary section. The Contents list on the opposite page shows how the Workbook follows the topics and syllabus of the Student's book, providing revision and extension of the material presented.

Pass Cambridge BEC Vantage Workbook includes the following features.

- **Grammar**

  Each grammar section begins with a clear and full explanation of the grammar presented in the Student's book. This is followed by practice exercises that test and develop students' knowledge. A full Answer key is provided at the back of the book.

- **Vocabulary**

  Each vocabulary section recycles key items from the *Pass Cambridge BEC Vantage Student's book* and introduces more key BEC Vantage vocabulary. A full Answer key is provided at the back of the book.

- **Review**

  There are two language reviews in *Pass Cambridge BEC Vantage Workbook:* after Units 5 and 10. Each review consists of one hundred grammar questions, which revise the grammar of the previous five units, and fifty multiple-choice vocabulary questions also based on the previous five units. A full Answer key is provided at the back of the book.

- **Writing**

  This reference section provides students with guidance on writing emails, formal letters and brief exam-style reports. The section includes a list of essential phrases useful to students not only in the examination but also in their professional lives.

Contents   Grammar   Vocabulary

		Grammar	Vocabulary
6	**Reporting** 34–37	Adjectives and adverbs Relative clauses	Change Reporting results Financial statements
7	**The workplace** 38–41	Modal verbs Passive	Health and safety Terms and conditions Disciplinary procedure In court
8	**Business travel** 42–45	Indirect questions Reported speech Verbs of suggesting	Flying Mathematical terms Expenses claims Letter writing
9	**People** 46–49	Gerunds Infinitives	Appraisals Trade unions Personnel Recruitment
10	**Marketing** 50–53	Conditional 1 (real) Conditional 2 (hypothetical)	Marketing Report writing
	Review 2 54–59	Review of Units 6–10	
	Writing 60–67	Letters and emails Formal letters Formal reports	**Answer key** 68–79

Management

Present simple

Form **The present simple has the following forms.**

*We **use** consultants.*
*She **doesn't authorise** payments.*
*Who **do** you **report** to?*
Who reports to you? (no auxiliary in questions asking for the subject)

Use **The present simple is used in the following ways.**

- to describe facts and permanent situations
  *All our contracts **comply** with EU law.*

- to describe routines
  *We **negotiate** salaries every autumn.*

Present continuous

Form **The present continuous has the following forms.**

*They**'re cutting** jobs in middle management.*
*I**'m not attending** the conference.*
*What **are** you **planning** to do about it?*

Use **The present continuous is used in the following ways.**

- to describe actions happening at the time of speaking
  *We**'re restructuring** our sales operation at the moment.*

- to describe temporary situations
  *A consultant **is working** with us for a few weeks.*

- to refer to future arrangements
  *We**'re relocating** to offices in Helsinki next year.*

Note! **We do not use the present continuous to express the following.**

routines *(usually, normally* etc.*)*   emotions *(like, love, hate)*
ownership *(own, have, need)*   opinions *(think, believe)*
senses *(see, hear, feel)*

Auxiliary verbs

Use **Auxiliary verbs (*do, have, be* and modals) are used in the following ways.**

- to form questions and negatives
  *We **don't** have any subsidiaries.*

- to show surprise or ask follow-up questions
  *He **doesn't have** any formal qualifications.*
  ***Doesn't** he?*

- to form question tags
  *He **doesn't speak** French, **does** he? (negative sentence + positive tag)*
  *They**'re working** today, **aren't** they? (positive sentence + negative tag)*
  *We **can't** attend the meeting tomorrow, **can** we?*

Grammar practice

Present simple

1 Complete the sentences with the correct present simple forms.

1 Our manager (*like*) _____likes_____ good team players.

2 We always (*do*) _____ a lot of on-the-job training.

3 Who (*you /report*) _____ to?

4 Why (*she /not /like*) _____ the new manager?

5 Who (*authorise*) _____ pay rises?

6 The assistant (*not /have*) _____ much responsibility.

7 They (*not /have*) _____ production meetings every week.

8 Who (*supervise*) _____ all the assistants and secretaries?

Present continuous

2 Complete the sentences with the correct present continuous forms.

1 We (*recruit*) *'re recruiting* some extra people for this project.

2 I (*try*) _____ to reduce our costs at the moment.

3 The company (*restructure*) _____ its management right now.

4 The team (*not /perform*) _____ very well this year.

5 Why (*you /schedule*) _____ a meeting for Monday?

6 Who (*take*) _____ care of the administration work while Sue's away?

7 We (*not /go*) _____ on the teamwork seminar next month.

8 They (*find*) _____ it hard to overcome the language problems in the team.

Present simple and continuous

3 Complete the email with correct present simple or present continuous forms.

◀ ▶ email	RE: Team-building

From : Jason O'Connell [joconnell@eurobrands.com]

Sent: Tuesday, September 10, 1.43 pm
To: Karen Majors
Subject: **RE: Team-building**

Thanks for your email, Karen. We (¹*go*) ___'re going___ ahead with the team-building weekend next month so you (²*need*) _____ to think about who you (³*want*) _____ to send on it from your team. Claudia (⁴*organise*) _____ the weekend. I (⁵*believe*) _____ she (⁶*negotiate*) _____ with a company in Scotland – one of those outdoor survival weekend-type things. It (⁷*not / sound*) _____ very cheap but I'm sure it'll be well worth the money – these things always (⁸*make*) _____ a huge difference to team spirit. Who usually (⁹*authorise*)_____ budgets for this kind of thing at your end? I (¹⁰*think*) _____ we should send as many people as possible this year. Let me know your numbers as soon as possible.

Question tags

4 Complete the sentences with the correct question tags.

1 You are going to the meeting on 25 May, _*aren't you?*_

2 He doesn't like working in large teams, _____

3 We won't meet the target, _____

4 They need to recruit more people, _____

5 Janice is organising the training, _____

6 We're not having a seminar this year, _____

Vocabulary practice

Meetings **1 Use the following words to complete the extract from an email below.**

> chief executive (CEO)   points of view   minutes   unanimous   casting vote
> counter-productive   summary   brainstorming   decision-making   objective

---

◄ ► **email**   RE: How's it going?

From :   Suzanna Gudinski [sgudinski@archetype.com]

Sent: Tuesday 3 April 11.36am
To: Alex Drummond
Subject: **RE: How's it going?**

Alex

Thanks for your email yesterday – great to hear from you. My first month with the new sales team has been good and I'm slowly getting used to how they work. You asked what's different here – well meetings for a start! They seem to have no definite [1] _objective_ or agenda to begin with and Michael Freed, the [2]_____ , calls meetings without any notice at all. He suddenly decides to have a [3]_____ session to come up with new ideas and calls an instant meeting. No-one is prepared or anything so we sit around, drink coffee and can't think of anything, which seems a bit [4]_____ to me. And the [5]_____ process is a bit strange too. Everyone puts forward their [6]_____ and then if there isn't [7]_____ agreement, it gets put to a vote. Michael has the [8]_____ , of course, so he usually gets what he wants at the end of the day and you wonder what the point of voting on it was. And there's no [9]_____ at the end of the meeting of what was agreed and I've never seen any formal written [10]_____ distributed to anyone after the meeting either. It's certainly all very different to how we used to do things but the department is very profitable so I guess Michael must know what he's doing. It's going to take a while for me to get ...

Management **2 Match the verbs with the nouns then use them to complete the sentences below.**

allocate ———————— the company structure
authorise ————————— resources
delegate   a vote
negotiate   a report
reorganise   a payment
submit   a task
cast   costs
control   a deal

1 We're reviewing how we _allocate resources_ in order to maximise productivity.
2 Every year she meets with the suppliers to _____ to save us a lot of money.
3 I'm afraid only the Head of Department is able to _____ over $500.
4 We're hoping to _____ in time for people to read it before the meeting.
5 They're trying to _____ , which will probably mean no pay rise this year.
6 Any directors not attending the board meeting can _____ by email.
7 They've hired a consultant to _____ and improve our processes.
8 He's a very 'hands-on' manager – he doesn't know how to _____ .

Abbreviations **3** **Match the abbreviations with the definitions.**

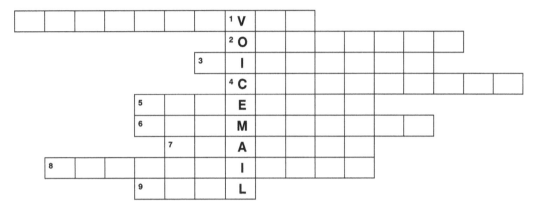

1 asap
2 AOB
3 enc.
4 etc.
5 SAE
6 c/o
7 cc
8 re.

a) enclosed documents
b) very quickly
c) with reference to
d) copy sent to
e) miscellaneous items on an agenda
f) sent care of someone else
g) and so on
h) enclosed pre-paid addressed envelope

Teamwork **4** **Use the clues below to complete the puzzle.**

¹ V
² O
3 I
⁴ C
5 E
6 M
7 A
8 I
9 L

1 something you are trying to achieve
2 training carried out while the employee works
3 diagram of a circle divided into segments
4 someone who is paid to advise management
5 programme of events / actions and times when they happen
6 person who is part of a team
7 person being taught how to do a job
8 someone who takes part in something
9 something you hope to achieve in the future

Word formation **5** **Complete the table then use the words to complete the sentences below.**

verb	noun	person	adjective
manage	_management_	manager	_managerial_
_____	administration		
_____	_____	assistant	assistant
organise	_____	organiser	_____
_____	_____	partner	partner
represent	_____	representative	representative
_____	analysis	_____	_____
_____	_____	supervisor	_____

1 She's got great _managerial_ skills. She always gets the best out of her staff.
2 The figures aren't very _____ of our performance last year.
3 He's retired but keeps a _____ role as a non-executive director.
4 She's really good at understanding figures – she's got a very _____ mind.
5 All the _____ in the department is done by our support staff.
6 We formed a _____ with one of our overseas agents.
7 I'd like you to _____ Ingrid with getting the project off the ground.
8 Peter can arrange the conference – he's got excellent _____ skills.

Customers

Past simple

Form   **The past simple has the following forms.**

*We **took** our clients to see the new factory.*
*Many customers **didn't attend** the product launch.*
*When **did** you **finalise** the deal?*

Use   **The past simple is used in the following ways.**

- to describe finished events
  *We **reorganised** our distribution two years ago.*
- to refer to definite or finished time periods
  *We **ran** some customer service training sessions in May.*

Present perfect

Form   **The present perfect has the following forms.**

*We **have reduced** our budget.*   *Our service **has been improving** lately.*
*I **haven't processed** the order yet.*   *He **hasn't been visiting** clients enough.*
***Have** they **renewed** the contract?*   *What **have** you **been working** on?*

Use   **The present perfect is used in the following ways.**

- to describe events that started in the past and are still continuing
  *The company **has been doing** business with them since 2006.*
- to refer to unfinished or indefinite time
  *They'**ve improved** their customer service a lot.*
- to describe changes that affect the present situation
  *We'**ve just opened** a new after-sales service centre.*

Note!   **The present perfect simple emphasises the product of an action while the present perfect continuous emphasises the process itself.**

*We'**ve increased** our customer base by 22 per cent this year.*
*We'**ve been spending** a lot of money on our sales outlets lately.*

Time references

Form   **Note the verb forms used with the following time references.**

- finished time (*ago, yesterday, last week /month /year, all dates*)
  *We **started** planning the launch six months **ago**.*
- unfinished time (*already, today, this week /month, for, since, yet, ever, never*)
  *I **haven't managed** to speak to the client **today**.*
- recent time (*recently, just, lately, in the last few minutes /days /weeks*)
  *She was at her desk but I **haven't seen** her **in the last few minutes**.*

Note!   **'for' is used with periods of time whereas 'since' is used with fixed points.**

*Barnard Design has been a customer of ours **for 12 years /since 2000**.*

Grammar practice

Past simple

1 Complete the sentences with the correct past simple forms.

1 We (*reorganise*) _____ the department last year.
2 What time (*the clients /arrive*) _____ this morning?
3 (*you /take*) _____ the client to the Grand Prix last week?
4 The customer (*not /be*) _____ happy with the level of service.
5 After some small talk, we (*get*) _____ down to business after lunch.
6 They (*take*) _____ the visitors shopping yesterday afternoon.
7 We (*not /want*) _____ to lose such a valued customer.
8 (*you /secure*) _____ a deal over dinner last night?
9 We (*not /finalise*) _____ the arrangements until yesterday.
10 The client (*not /have*) _____ time to go to the theatre on Friday.

Past simple and present perfect

2 Complete the dialogue with the correct form of the verbs in brackets.

Sven — So, Mr Chaing, you (¹*come*) _____'ve come_____ in this morning to talk about a start-up loan for a small business.

Mr Chaing — That's right, yes. I (²*come*) _____ last month ...

Sven — And you (³*speak*) _____ to my colleague Joanne Watts. She (⁴*pass*) _____ your application on to me a few days ago. What (⁵*she /say*) _____ to you?

Mr Chaing — She just (⁶*give*) _____ me some general advice on applying for the loan and (⁷*ask*) _____ me to fill in some forms.

Sven — Which I see you (⁸*already /do*) _____ . That's great. I see she also (⁹*ask*) _____ you to prepare a business plan, which we (¹⁰*already /receive*) _____ . (¹¹*you /find*) _____ it hard to do the plan?

Mr Chaing — Well, I (¹²*not /do*) _____ it on my own. A friend of mine, who owns his own company, (¹³*help*) _____ me with it.

Sven — That's very useful, knowing someone running their own company. How long (¹⁴*he /be*) _____ in business?

Mr Chaing — About five years now. That's where I (¹⁵*get*) _____ the idea from to start my own company.

Sven — That's often the case. Now (¹⁶*you /do*) _____ a cash flow forecast yet? It says here that we (¹⁷*not /receive*) _____ one.

Mr Chaing — No, but I (¹⁸*bring*) _____ it with me ... here it is.

Sven — Excellent. So, let's have a look at these figures, shall we?

Time references

3 Use the following time references to complete the sentences below.

never	since	for	already	ever	yet	recently	ago

1 We've ___never___ had any problems doing business with them.
2 We've been banking with them _____ over 22 years.
3 We haven't been having as many complaints _____ .
4 We've _____ transferred the money to your account.
5 Have you finished the customer satisfaction survey _____?
6 Have you _____ taken a client to a sporting event?
7 We opened our customer service call centre two years _____ .
8 Entertainment budgets have increased _____ the merger last year.

Vocabulary practice

Corporate hospitality

1 Use the clues below to find 14 ways of entertaining clients in the puzzle.

E	V	S	S	Y	D	N	E	Y	Y	O	E
S	I	G	H	T	S	E	E	I	N	G	T
T	G	C	O	N	C	E	R	T	F	A	C
H	G	O	P	E	G	O	L	E	O	L	R
E	R	L	P	G	F	P	P	N	O	L	I
A	A	D	I	N	N	E	R	N	T	E	C
T	N	R	N	L	W	R	U	I	B	R	K
R	D	U	G	K	R	A	G	S	A	Y	E
E	P	G	F	O	O	T	B	A	L	L	T
S	R	B	T	E	N	N	Y	P	T	S	R
E	I	P	H	O	R	S	E	R	A	C	E
P	X	G	R	G	O	L	F	O	P	E	R

1 ~~see the famous sights of a city~~
2 a meal at a nice restaurant
3 a sport played with an oval ball
4 seeing Manchester United, for example
5 a musical by Mozart or Puccini, for example
6 a place to see a play by Shakespeare
7 an event where people bet on horses
8 an event with live music
9 visiting interesting stores
10 a place where paintings are displayed
11 Wimbledon, for example
12 a sport where both teams wear white
13 a game with clubs and 18 holes
14 a race with Formula One cars

Word formation

2 Complete the table then use the words to complete the sentences below.

verb	noun	person
partner	_partnership_	partner
claim	claim	_____
_____	negotiation	_____
consume	_____	consumer
_____	distribution	_____
host	_____	host

1 The joint venture has been a very profitable _partnership_ .
2 A sports event isn't the best place to _____ an important contract.
3 He's a terrible _____ . He leaves guests on their own and talks to colleagues.
4 Our overseas _____ is handled by a Dutch transport company.
5 Working for an insurance company, I know that a lot of _____ don't tell the whole truth when they fill in accident report forms.
6 Customers have increased their _____ of organic food by 16 per cent.

3 Match the verbs with the nouns to complete the table.

	customers	relationships	orders	objectives	contracts
finalise	✗	✗	✓	✓	✓
meet					
win					
establish					
cancel					
manage					

4 Use the following words to complete the letter below.

> colleagues   substantial   satisfaction   after-sales service
> backlog   valued customer   inconvenience   value for money

Mrs Janet Walberg
MetroTechnics
1044 Corn Fields
San Diego
CA 92122

2 July 2011

Re: **Order No. 2001036MT**

Dear Mrs Walberg

Thank you for your letter of 27 June. We are very sorry that your order has not been sent. This is because of the large numbers of orders we have received lately, which have caused a [1] _backlog_ . This has not been helped by the fact that several of my [2] _____ are off sick at the moment.

We will despatch the parts very shortly. We hope this is to your [3] _____ and the delay has not caused you too much [4] _____ .

As you are a [5] _____ , we would like to offer you a [6] _____ saving on our extended warranty option. For as little as $200, you could enjoy our full [7] _____ for four years on all parts. This special price offers excellent [8] _____ as well as peace of mind. Please call me if you would like to take advantage of this offer.

Yours truly

5 Use the following information to write a reply to the letter. Write 120–140 words.

> Jenny
> Could you reply to this letter from Peter Carson at West Coast
> Electrics for me and include the following points?
> – Ask him to confirm the delivery date.
> – Add another 2 motors to the order (cat no. 2203E) – if we can.
> – Agree to the extended warranty.
> – Ask Peter to send a new invoice with those changes.
> Thanks

Commerce

Future arrangements

Form **Future arrangements can be expressed in the following ways.**

We're getting a new delivery in tomorrow morning.
The train leaves at 6.30 tomorrow evening.

Use **These forms are used in the following ways.**

- to describe events that have been arranged
  The shipment is arriving on 16 October.
- to refer to fixed timetables or schedules
  The plane lands at 10.40pm local time.

Note! **Will is not used to describe future arrangements.**

We will meet our agents next week.
We're meeting our agents next week.

Future intentions

Form **Future intentions can be expressed in the following ways.**

We're going to issue a final demand if they don't pay soon.
I think we'll pay by letter of credit.

Use **These forms are used in the following ways.**

- to describe existing intentions
  We're going to set up a direct debit agreement.
- to express spontaneous intentions
  A mistake is seen on an invoice: *Oh no. We'll have to issue a credit note.*

Predictions

Form **Predictions can be made in the following ways.**

The ship's going to be ready to leave in the next day or two.
The goods will arrive late if the bad weather continues.
Shipping costs are likely to go up in future. (also bound to, set to, unlikely to)

Use **These forms are used in the following ways.**

- for spoken predictions based on knowledge / evidence
  We're going to have problems getting the order ready in time.
- for spontaneous spoken predictions
  A dockers' strike? This means our shipment'll be delayed.
- for written predictions in newspapers / magazines
  The strong pound will hit UK exports into Europe.

Note! **Modal verbs can also be used to express uncertainty about the future.**

There could be a delay at customs.
The consignment might not leave Rotterdam until Friday.

Grammar practice

Arrangements

1 Choose the most appropriate verb form to complete each sentence.

1 The ticket says the plane *lands / is landing* at 18.25.

2 I *pick / 'm picking* them up from the train station on Friday.

3 We *send / 're sending* the cheque tomorrow.

4 The early morning train *doesn't arrive / isn't arriving* until 7.40.

5 I *open / 'm opening* a new account next week.

6 I *see / 'm seeing* a financial adviser on Monday.

7 The accountants *start / are starting* the audit next Wednesday.

8 The goods *go / are going* through customs today.

Spontaneous intentions

2 Match the questions and statements with the responses.

1 Is the money in the account yet?   **a)** I'll just check my diary.

2 I'd like to have a credit card, please.   **b)** I'll just call up your details and see.

3 Can I put some money in my account?   **c)** OK. I'll get an application form.

4 What's your current interest rate?   **d)** One moment. I'll check the balance.

5 How much is in the account?   **e)** I'll get a copy of our terms and conditions.

6 Can I make an appointment for Monday? **f)** We'll have to order that much currency.

7 Can I change £500 into dollars, please? **g)** Certainly. I'll get you a paying-in slip.

Futures

3 Complete the dialogue with the correct future forms.

Faiza	Michael. Nice to see you again. Come in. How's business?
Michael	Hi Faiza. Business isn't too good, I'm afraid. That's why I'm here.
Faiza	OK. Well, sit down and let's see what we (¹*do*) _'re going to do_ about it.
Michael	Thanks. I (²*just / get*) _____ some papers out and then I can show you what the problem is.
Faiza	OK. I (³*get*) _____ my glasses. How many people do you have working for you now?
Michael	Thirty-six but two more people (⁴*start*) _____ on Monday.
Faiza	Wow. That's great. Thing are growing really quickly.
Michael	It gets busy at this time of year. It always does about now. It's the nature of the business.
Faiza	(⁵*you / take*) _____ on any more people on over the summer?
Michael	I'd like to but I don't think we (⁶*be*) _____ able to afford it. But without the extra workers, we (⁷*not / fulfil*) _____ all the orders we already have, not to mention any new ones.
Faiza	Oh, I see.
Michael	I (⁸*definitely / need*) _____ to raise some finance somehow over the summer so I can take on more workers. And that's why I'm here. Do you think the bank (⁹*lend*) _____ me some more money?
Faiza	Whatever they do, they (¹⁰*want*) _____ to take a close look at these figures to see how your business is doing.
Michael	I know. I (¹¹*see*) _____ my bank manager next week. I've got an appointment on Thursday. So I thought maybe you could look at these figures for me and advise me on what to say at the bank.
Faiza	Sure. I (¹²*see*) _____ what I can do.
Michael	Thanks, Faiza. It (¹³*not / be*) _____ easy on Monday and I think I (¹⁴*need*) _____ all the help I can get.

Vocabulary practice

1 Complete the word diagram with the following banking words.

> ~~balance~~   payee   credit   deduct   paying-in slip   creditor
> transaction   counterfoil   adviser   interest   advice note
> statement   cashier   deposit   banker   debit

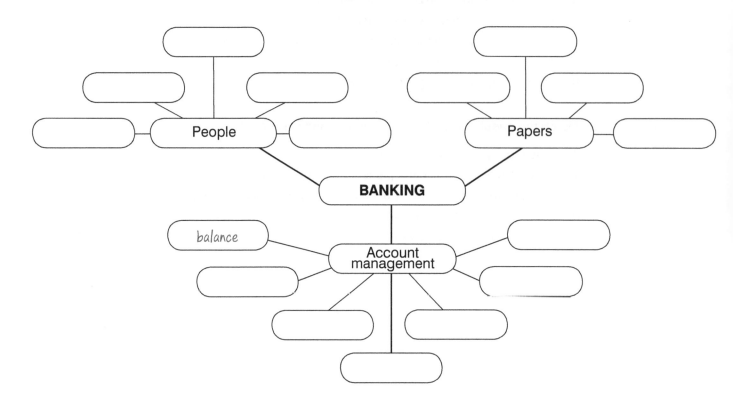

Banking
services

2 Match the banking services with the definitions.

1	loan	a)	place where you leave money to earn interest
2	statement	b)	specific sum of money lent by a bank
3	transfer	c)	regular automatic payment from your account
4	cheque	d)	limited amount of credit on your current account
5	current account	e)	helpful information about managing your money
6	savings account	f)	printed, signed paper that you use to pay for things instead of money
7	direct debit	g)	printed record of all your account's transactions
8	standing order	h)	account from which you can withdraw money quickly
9	financial advice	i)	movement of money from one account to another
10	overdraft	j)	order giving access to your account to pay bills etc.

Payments

3 Match the payments with the payers and payees.

	payer	payment	payee
1	a tax payer	customs duty	the government
2	a bank	income tax	shareholders
3	an importer	bank charges	an account holder
4	the government	interest on savings	a bank
5	an account holder	a dividend	a tax payer
6	a company	tax relief	the government

Odd one out

4 Which word does not go with the word in capital letters?

1 BANK			
~~year~~	transfer	loan	statement
2 FINANCIAL			
adviser	services	year	payment
3 TAX			
deductible	return	transaction	free
4 INTEREST			
free	rate	discount	payment
5 DIRECT			
debit	cash	transfer	costs
6 CASH			
sale	purchase	price	note
7 ACCOUNT			
number	code	manager	holder
8 FIXED			
rate	condition	term	cost
9 CREDIT			
card	note	cheque	transfer
10 BANK			
charge	duty	code	manager

Importing goods

5 Put the following stages of an import process in the correct order.

☐ **a)** The distributor delivers the goods and invoices the customer.

☑ **b)** The customer places the order with the local distributor.

☐ **c)** The overseas supplier produces the goods and ships them.

☐ **d)** The distributor issues a letter of credit or bank draft to the supplier.

☐ **e)** The distributor orders the goods from the overseas supplier.

☐ **f)** The customer receives the goods and pays the distributor.

☐ **g)** The goods arrive and go through customs.

Dealing with suppliers

6 Match the verbs with the nouns then use them to complete the sentences below.

deliver	haulage
fill in	goods
pay	a consignment
arrange	import duty
ship	a delivery note
negotiate with	a supplier

1 We usually _deliver goods_ by courier.

2 We always _____ with a local logistics company.

3 Don't forget to _____ and check all the other paperwork.

4 We had to _____ to increase our margins on the order.

5 The customs won't release the goods until we _____ .

6 We can _____ next week as there's a boat leaving Rotterdam.

Brands

Determiners

Form **Countable and uncountable nouns have the following forms.**

countable	uncountable
a brand	~~*an*~~ *advertising*
two brands	~~*two*~~ *advertising~~s~~*
	Uncountable nouns take a singular verb.

Use **Determiners are used in the following ways.**

countable nouns

*We have **some** new brochures.*
*There are **a lot of** features.*
*There weren't **many** enquiries.*
*We only have **a few** samples.*
***All** our products are branded.*
*We don't have **any** brochures.*
***Both** logos use the same colours.*
***Each** / **Every** campaign is different.*

uncountable nouns

*There is **some** brand awareness.*
*We did **a lot of** public relations work.*
*There wasn't **much** interest in the product.*
*There is **a little** stock left.*
*One agency does **all** our advertising.*
*Have you done **any** advertising yet?*

Articles

Use **The indefinite article (*a* / *an*) is used in the following ways.**

*   to refer to general singular countable nouns
    *It's **a** very well-known **brand**.*
    *Versace is **an** expensive **brand** of Italian clothing.*

*   to refer to jobs
    *I'm **a brand manager**.*

The definite article (*the*) is used in the following ways.

*   to refer to nouns already mentioned or defined
    *We can change the logo. **The old one** looks a little bit boring.*

*   to refer to nouns that are unique
    *We're selling more and more products on **the Internet**.*

*   to refer to superlatives
    *Nokia is one of **the most popular brands** of mobile phone.*

No article (Ø) is used in the following situations.

*   to refer to proper names (companies, sectors, cities, countries)
    *I work for **Motorola** in **Singapore**.*
    *(But **the** is used in The United States, The Republic of China, etc.)*
    *Sales are good in **the United Arab Emirates**.*

*   to refer to general uncountable or general plural nouns
    *We need to increase **market awareness**.*

Note! **If an adjective is used before a general noun, no article is required.**

We need to increase sales.
We need to increase annual sales.

Grammar practice

Determiners **1 Choose the correct word to complete each sentence.**

1 The product doesn't enjoy *much* / *many* brand awareness.

2 The supermarket doesn't have *some* / *any* own-brand products.

3 We'll have to make a *few* / *little* more concessions on price.

4 There aren't *some* / *any* copyright problems with the new advert.

5 *Each* / *All* of our competitors tend to stick to the same brands.

6 We have two suppliers in Italy. *Both* / *All* of them are located near international airports.

7 We've only had a *few* / *little* feedback from our markets so far.

8 There are *much* / *a lot of* counterfeit products on the market.

9 We have stores in *every* / *all* major town in the country.

10 I've got most of the forecasts but I still don't have *some* / *any* of them.

2 Find and correct the mistake in each line of the text.

1 Steve. Please find <u>some</u> attached copies of the new packaging	*the*
2 design. There are a little small changes to the design including	_____
3 making the logo bigger to increase the brand awareness. We've	_____
4 also changed the text a few in places to make it shorter so it	_____
5 fits in with an overall design better. Could you check the text	_____
6 very carefully – both time it's come back from the printers	_____
7 there's been a mistake in it. We haven't got many time before this	_____
8 goes to print so I'd be grateful for many comments as soon	_____
9 as possible. We need to provide an information about exactly	_____
10 how much units we want to print. Is 250,000 OK?	_____

Articles **3 Complete the email with *a, an, the* or no article (Ø).**

◄ ► email	RE: Loyalty card

From :	Elizabeth Conroy [jeconroy@citystores.com]
Sent:	Friday September 21, 2011 5:16 pm
To:	Connor Murrell
Subject:	**RE: Loyalty card**

Connor

Thanks for your email. I think ¹ *the* loyalty card is ² ___ great idea. As you know, we're speeding up ³ ___ process of selling more own-brand products so ⁴ ___ loyalty card would also help to increase ⁵ ___ brand awareness. We could also offer ⁶ ___ extra points on selected products as ⁷ ___ extra promotional tool. ⁸ ___ good loyalty points scheme will give us ⁹ ___ added flexibility in terms of ¹⁰ ___ pricing too. You said you'd done ¹¹ ___ cost analysis for implementing such ¹² ___ scheme. I'd like to see ¹³ ___ figures as soon as possible. I'll need ¹⁴ ___ idea of how long it would take to put into ¹⁵ ___ action too.

Vocabulary practice

Global brands **1 Match the brands with the nationalities and products.**

1	Vodafone	Japanese	telecommunications
2	Dell	British	cosmetics
3	BMW	German	computer games
4	IKEA	Italian	cars
5	Benetton	Finnish	mobile phones
6	Sony	US	clothes
7	Nokia	French	furniture
8	L'Oréal	Swedish	computers

Buying decisions **2 Match each speaker with a reason for buying a certain brand of computer.**

user-friendliness   price   image   performance   after-sales service

1 I needed a computer but I didn't want to spend a lot on something that could do all kinds of things I didn't need to do. I was more interested in getting the best deal available.

2 Brands are very important for some people but not me. I'm more concerned about how powerful it is and what it can do. I don't want to pay this much money for something which is out of date in a few months' time.

3 Let's face it, computers go wrong no matter how great they look in the shop. The important thing is what happens when it goes wrong at home. What's the helpline like? What kind of support do you get?

4 I'm not very good with technology and find all the features very confusing but this one seems really straightforward. So I can get things done without having to read the instructions several times.

5 All my friends have PCs that look exactly the same. I wanted something different so when I saw the iMac, I thought it looked great and I just fell in love with it. It looks so stylish on my desk at home.

Odd one out **3 Which word is the odd one out?**

1	buy	advertise	purchase	acquire
2	status	image	power	characteristics
3	admit	convince	persuade	encourage
4	agenda	issue	aim	goal
5	values	ethics	conditions	ideals
6	proponents	investors	supporters	customers
7	slogan	policy	logo	brand
8	finance	borrowing	funding	insurance
9	members	companies	shareholders	owners
10	concerns	policies	ground rules	practices

4 Match the verbs with the nouns and then use them to complete the sentences below. You might need to change the form of the words.

lay out	change
withhold	ground rules
comply with	loyalty
bring about	funding
run	ideals
stretch	policies
carry	a business
provide	product lines
cling to	healthcare
create	a brand

1 We need to _lay out ground rules_ about how we're going to do business together before we sign an official agreement with them.

2 The bank _____ because we hadn't been able to make interest payments on our existing credit agreements.

3 In order to win investment from the Co-operative Bank, you need to _____ on ethical issues such as fair trade and animal rights.

4 The bank uses its position as a shareholder to _____ in the companies that it invests in.

5 The Co-operative Bank demonstrates that it's possible to _____ both profitably and ethically.

6 Many supermarkets have _____ by opening up banks and selling credit cards to their customers.

7 The Co-operative supermarkets _____ that follow their own ethical guidelines by being fair trade or grown on co-operative farms.

8 The Co-operative Group also _____ and insurance on an ethical basis.

9 Many people believe that if you _____ in business, you can never build a very successful company.

10 Some companies see ethical policies and campaigns as a way of _____ in their existing customers as well as attracting new ones.

5 Use the following words to complete the email below.

feedback	brand loyalty	pricing policy	premium
loss-leader	household name	brand awareness	

◄ ► [email]   RE: S220 feedback

From :	Julie Bain [jules@metrotek.com]
Sent:	Monday September 3 1:16 pm
To:	Samantha Morgan
Subject:	**RE: S220 feedback**

Sam

Here's a quick summary of the market ¹ _feedback_ on the S220. As expected, a lot of the sales are through existing customers, with 65% of them having upgraded to the S220, so ² _____ seems high. But only 15% of non-current customers had heard of the S200 series so we need to build up ³ _____ . I mean 15% doesn't exactly make the S220 a ⁴ _____ , does it?

I think we need to review our ⁵ _____ and think about special promotional discounts and other targeted offers to help grow market share. I know the S220 cost a lot to develop and I don't want to turn it into a ⁷ _____ but I really think we're charging too much of a price ⁸ _____ to establish a wide enough customer base.

Let me know what you think.

Jules

Facilities

Comparatives and superlatives

Form   **Adjectives have the following comparative and superlative forms.**

	adjective	comparative	superlative
single syllable	*new*	*new**er***	*the new**est***
-ly endings	*ear~~ly~~*	*earl**ier***	*the earl**iest***
multi-syllable	*attractive*	***more** attractive*	***the most** attractive*
		***less** attractive*	***the least** attractive*
irregular	*good*	**better**	**the best**
	bad	**worse**	**the worst**

Adverbs have the following comparative and superlative forms.

	adverb	comparative	superlative
all adverbs	*efficiently*	***more** efficiently*	***the most** efficiently*
		***less** efficiently*	***the least** efficiently*

Note!   **Comparisons of adjectives and adverbs can be made in two ways.**

*For our company, Turin **is** a **better** location **than** Milan.*
*For our company, Milan **isn't as good** a location **as** Turin.*

Participles

Form   **Participles have the following forms.**

- present participles
  *Their new headquarters is a **fascinating** building.*
  ***Wanting** to save money, the company moved out of Shanghai.*
- past participles
  *All **relocated** staff were given travel vouchers.*
- perfect participles
  ***Having looked** at locations for six months, they decided on the Melbourne site.*
  ***Not having seen** the relocation report, she couldn't comment on it.*

Use   **Participles can be used in the following ways.**

- as an adjective before a noun
  *Brussels is our main **processing** centre.*
  *Our cleaning company now has a **renegotiated** contract.*
- in compound adjectives
  *Leaving the Sydney office was a very **short-sighted** move.*
  *The new equipment will have **long-lasting** benefits for our staff.*
- with adverbs and superlatives
  *The **attractively laid out** offices are very pleasant to work in.*
  *It's one of **the fastest growing** areas for business investment.*

Participles can also follow nouns in relative clauses.

*The network (that was) **installed** last month has been very reliable.*

Grammar practice

Comparatives and superlatives

1 **Complete the extract from a report on three locations for a UK sales office with the correct comparative or superlative form of the words in brackets.**

Findings

Of the three locations, Cambridge, Ealing and Guildford, Cambridge is certainly by far (¹cheap) _the cheapest_ in terms of basic annual rent. However, it is also (²far)

_____ from the centre of London (about 100km). The Ealing location is situated in the Greater London area and of the three sites offers (³easy) _____ access to the centre of London by underground. Although Guildford is 50km from London, it is almost as (⁴expensive) _____ the Ealing site. Feedback from staff likely to move to the UK office shows that living in London is one of (⁵important) _____ factors in their decision to relocate. Culturally, Ealing is the (⁶attractive) _____ of the three locations, offering easy access to (⁷good)

_____ cinema, music, shows, international theatre and sightseeing. Although Ealing would be (⁸expensive) _____ solution for the company, it would mean UK sales executives would be very close to (⁹large) _____ proportion of our UK customers. This would mean they could operate (¹⁰efficiently) _____ and offer a (¹¹good) _____ service than if they were in Cambridge or Guildford.

Participles

2 **Choose the correct participle to complete each sentence.**

1 *Mass-produced*/*Mass-producing* goods are not always the cheapest.
2 Moving into our new offices will be really *exciting*/*excited*.
3 Virus protection is essential for *networked*/*networking* computers.
4 Many *returning*/*having returned* expatriates experience culture shock.
5 *Having finished*/*Finishing* the plant in May, we installed the machinery in June.
6 We're doing a cost-benefit analysis of several *interesting*/*interested* sites.
7 The money *invested*/*investing* in the new machinery was well spent.
8 The *newly-constructed*/*newly-constructing* warehouse improved distribution.
9 *Having relocated*/*Relocating* our production, we saw an increase in productivity.
10 The company is *interesting*/*interested* in a site just outside Melbourne.
11 We've had a good return on our *invested*/*investing* capital.

3 **Match the words with the participles to form compound adjectives.**

1 short   a) conditioned
2 long   b) sighted
3 mass   c) running
4 air   d) automated
5 fully   e) lasting
6 long   f) produced

Vocabulary practice

1 Use the clues below to complete the crossword.

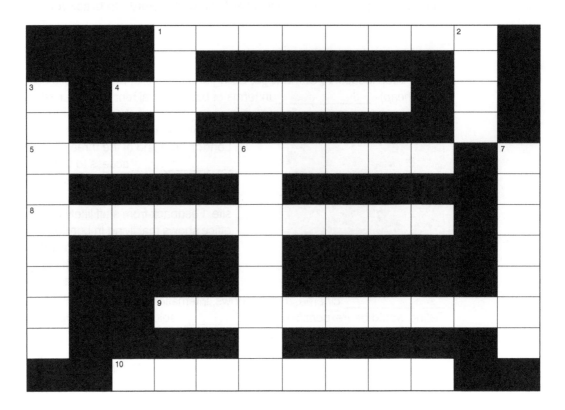

▶ **Across**

1 buildings owned by a company (8)
4 building where goods are manufactured (7)
5 firm that builds new buildings under contract (10)
8 what is needed to finance new buildings and equipment (10)
9 the right to use a building for a limited amount of time (9)
10 putting pre-manufactured components together (8)

▼ **Down**

1 collective name for all the machinery in a factory (5)
2 place where a building is located (4)
3 collective noun for lots of machines (9)
6 use machines to do work instead of people (8)
7 improve facilities to a higher grade (7)

2 Put the following stages of building new premises in the correct order.

- ❑ **a)** The blueprints are finalised and sent to potential contractors.
- ❑ **b)** The company decides to invest in new premises and selects a site.
- ❑ **c)** Construction work begins on the site.
- ❑ **d)** The contractors submit tenders for the contract.
- ❑ **e)** The factory is officially handed over to the company.
- ❑ **f)** The company allocates a budget and commissions an architect.
- ☑ **g)** A company finds it is running in excess of capacity and thinks about expansion.
- ❑ **h)** The company chooses a contractor and signs contracts.
- ❑ **i)** The new factory is completed and new machinery is fitted.

3 Complete the word diagram with the following words and phrases.

motorways public transport grants skills road access
availability of workers local wage levels renovation costs
waterways running costs employment law airports rent

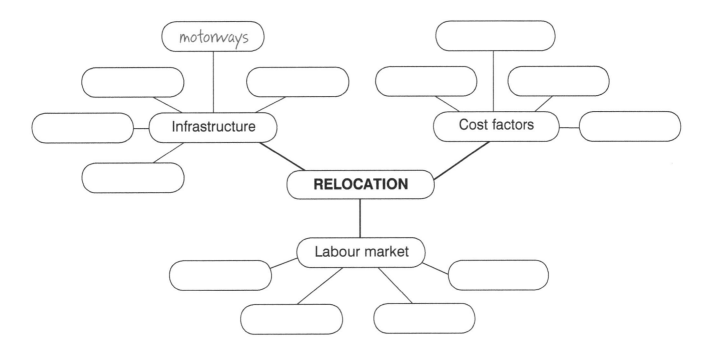

4 Write the following report phrases in the correct groups below.

The purpose of this report is ...
It is suggested that ...
This report aims to ...
It was decided that ...
We would suggest that ...
It was felt that ...
It is proposed that ...
No decision was reached regarding ...
This report sets out to ...

Introduction	Conclusion	Recommendation
The purpose of this report is ...		

Report writing **4 A US multinational is considering locating a new assembly plant in your city/town. Write a 120–140 word report on why your city/town would be suitable for the plant and make a recommendation as to the best site for the new plant.**

Review unit 1 (1–5)

Grammar

1 Complete the dialogue with the correct present simple or present continuous forms.

John   Have you finished that order yet?

Karl   Which one?

John   The one to our Danish distributor. He's been on the phone asking about it. Is it ready?

Karl   Oh right. That one. I think it's almost ready. Claudia has it. She (¹*just/finish*) _____ off the shipping papers at this moment.

John   Who (²*you/ship*) _____ the order with? NorShip, as usual?

Karl   No, we're not. We (³*use*) _____ a company called TradeLine Shipping this time.

John   TradeLine? We (⁴*not/use*) _____ them normally ...

Karl   I know we don't. But they're a new shipping agent and they (⁵*have*) _____ some really good prices right now. They (⁶*try*) _____ to build up a customer base so their prices are low at the moment.

John   But are they reliable?

Karl   Well, they (⁷*seem*) _____ to be reliable so far. We (⁸*give*) _____ them some small orders to see how they handle them. If they do OK, then we'll think about using them for some larger, more important orders in the future.

John   What kind of orders (⁹*you/send*) _____ with them at the moment?

Karl   Only orders up to €50,000. And most of them are to our European distributors, through Rotterdam mainly.

John   OK. That sounds fine. When (¹⁰*the ship/leave*) _____ harbour?

Karl   Well, according to the schedule. It (¹¹*leave*) _____ tomorrow afternoon, at 5pm, I (¹²*think*) _____ .

John   And will the papers be ready in time?

Karl   They should be, yes.

John   And is the cargo already on board?

Karl   They (¹³*load*) _____ it this afternoon.

John   Make sure you get confirmation that the cargo is safely on board. We (¹⁴*not/want*) _____ the ship to sail without it.

Karl   The agent (¹⁵*call*) _____ me at 4pm this afternoon to confirm that loading has been completed.

John   That's great. Well done.

2 Choose the correct option to complete each sentence.

1 We don't have *many/much* time before the trade fair.
2 I have a *few/little* brochures left in stock.
3 *Each/All* of our sales agents get a monthly product update.
4 I'd like *some/any* information on the new product, please.
5 We had *a lot of/much* problems with the projector.
6 A lot of people visited the stand, *both/all* attracted by our free samples.
7 We need to spend *a few/little* bit more on our advertising.
8 I've got *some/a* good news for you.
9 How *much/many* participants are attending the session?
10 We don't want *some/any* problems with the export licence.

3 Complete the email with the correct past simple or present perfect forms.

◄ ► email	RE: Project Management Training

From:	Connie Hedger [hedger@net-connect.com]
Sent:	Wednesday 31 October 4.12pm
To:	Fiona Deschamps
Subject:	**RE: Project Management Training**

Fiona

Thanks for your email and for booking a room for the Project Management Training session. I (¹*already/send*) _____ the confirmation of the room and times to the participants. I (²*invite*) _____ eighteen people but some of them (³*not/respond*) _____ yet so I'm afraid I don't have the final numbers for you. I (⁴*speak*) _____ to James yesterday and he (⁵*say*) _____ he can't make it, which is a bit of a shame as I (⁶*plan*) _____ the session for people like him. He (⁷*do*) _____ a lot of project management this year so far and he (⁸*even/ask*) _____ me several times for training support. To be honest, I'm really annoyed with him as he (⁹*know*) _____ about this session for months and yet three weeks ago he (¹⁰*arrange*) _____ a trip to Amsterdam! Of course he (¹¹*not/mention*) _____ the trip when we (¹²*speak*) _____ yesterday. I only (¹³*find*) _____ out about it this morning from Jo, his PA. As you can imagine, I (¹⁴*be*) _____ really angry when Jo (¹⁵*tell*) _____ me he wouldn't be here. But that's James for you.

4 Are the *italicised* words correct in these sentences? If not, write the correct words in the gaps. If the sentence is correct, write OK.

1 We changed the brand name six months *for*. _____
2 I haven't finished the report *now*. _____
3 We've been doing business with them *for* six years. _____
4 Have you *ever* been to the Expo trade fair? _____
5 The products have been on the market *since* three years. _____
6 She's *already* finished the posters. _____
7 We've been selling them *since* over 12 years. _____
8 I haven't seen her *lately*. _____
9 I've *not ever* been to the Paris office. _____
10 The new brochures arrived half an hour *ago*. _____

5 Complete the email with the most appropriate future forms.

email	RE: Japanese visitors

From:	Janice Theismann [janicet@mulligans.co.uk]
Sent:	Tuesday 9 January 11.44am
To:	Tom Lee
Subject:	**RE: Japanese visitors**

Tom

Just a quick email to let you know about arrangements for the Japanese visitors next week. I (¹be) _'ll be / 'm going to be_ out of the office for most of today so if you want to speak to me, you (²have) _____ to call me on my mobile. Sarah (³type) _____ up all the details later, but here are the main points:

Monday 9 July

Mr Suzuki and his three colleagues (⁴arrive) _____ in the morning. They (⁵fly) _____ with BA and the plane (⁶land) _____ at 9.45. Stella Nicholls (⁷pick) _____ them up from Heathrow airport. I don't know – but they (⁸want) _____ to go straight to their hotel first. If they do, then they probably (⁹not/get) _____ here until about 12.00, so we (¹⁰go) _____ straight to lunch. John Statham and Millicent Sharma (¹¹both/come) _____ for lunch. We (¹²go) _____ to the Plaza Hotel. (¹³you/have) _____ time to join us? I don't know how long we (¹⁴be) _____ so I haven't arranged any meetings until about 3.00. We (¹⁵meet) _____ our sales team at 3.00. If we do finish lunch earlier, then (¹⁶take) _____ them on a factory tour.

6 Complete the dialogue with the correct comparative and superlative forms.

Björn So, shall we start the appraisal with a look at last year's performance? How do you think you did?

Lucy Overall, I think I did (¹good) _____ than the year before. I know sales weren't (²good) _____ we've ever had but I think market conditions were (³tough) _____ they've been for years.

Björn In what way?

Lucy Customers were a lot (⁴careful) _____ with their budgets. Our feedback showed that they were just (⁵happy) _____ with our products as before. They just didn't have the money to buy more of them.

Björn So how did you deal with the market conditions?

Lucy Well, with sales down, we tried to work (⁶efficiently) _____ before and cut our production costs.

Björn Did it work?

Lucy Well, we achieved (⁷high) _____ margins we'd had for years. We reduced costs by 6% but quality levels weren't (⁸good) _____ in the previous six months.

Björn Why was that?

Lucy Well, we used (⁹experienced) _____ workers from a local agency so more mistakes were made than (¹⁰early) _____ in the year.

Björn That's a worry. What did you do about it?

7 **Choose the correct participles to complete the dialogue.**

Kelly   Hi, Miguel. How's the new advertising campaign going?

Miguel   Fine. A lot of people seem very ¹*interesting/interested* in the new product and we've had some really positive feedback from the ²*targeting/targeted* research we did.

Kelly   That's great news. Everyone seems to think that the new product is a big risk for some reason. I don't understand it.

Miguel   Well, I suppose it is a ³*newly-developing/newly-developed* product, which is always a bit of a risk. And it's a new market, too.

Kelly   But it's such a ⁴*fast-growing/fast-grown* market that you should be able to hit your sales targets OK.

Miguel   I know. ⁵*Receiving/Having received* all the sales forecasts, I think it'll do really well. I'm a bit worried that senior management won't give us the advertising budget though.

Kelly   It'll be very ⁶*short-sighting/short-sighted* of them if they don't.

Miguel   I know that and you know that, but try telling senior management! I'm convinced it'll be money very ⁷*well-investing/well-invested* in the medium to long term. ⁸*Doing/Having done* a lot of the research myself, I know how big the need is for just this kind of product ...

Kelly   But they won't approve a ⁹*mass-marketing/mass-marketed* campaign, right?

Miguel   That's my worry. Maybe the project will be more ¹⁰*interesting/interested* for them when they see some of the early sales figures. You never know.

8 **Complete the extract from a report with a, an, the or no article (Ø).**

> **Findings**
>
> Our new San Diego production facility should be completed by 17 June. Sanco, Inc., ¹ _the_ construction company building the facility, has confirmed that ² _____ basic shell of the building is almost complete. They are hoping to begin ³ _____ fitting machinery within ⁴ _____ three weeks.
>
> However, one of ⁵ _____ few problems we are having is ⁶ _____ purchase of ⁷ _____ suitable cookers. Originally we had ⁸ _____ Italian supplier in mind but we couldn't agree on ⁹ _____ terms.
>
> We have now found another supplier in ¹⁰ _____ UK, which is one of ¹¹ _____ best known British manufacturers of industrial cookers. We are confident this new supplier can deliver ¹² _____ high level of ¹³ _____ quality, but there will be ¹⁴ _____ short delay as ¹⁵ _____ deal was only reached at the last minute.

Vocabulary

Complete each sentence with the correct option.

1 This _____ here shows exactly how our payment processing works.
   a) graph   **b)** flow chart   **c)** pie chart

2 We had to get a bank _____ to finance the new machinery.
   a) credit   **b)** finance   **c)** loan

3 The market was flooded with cheap _____ products from abroad.
   a) genuine   **b)** bona fide   **c)** counterfeit

4 All our products come with a standard one-year _____ .
   a) warranty   **b)** shelf life   **c)** contract

5 The head of department will have to _____ the payment.
   a) authorise   **b)** summarise   **c)** analyse

6 I'm afraid delivery will be late because we have a _____ of orders.
   a) back date   **b)** batch   **c)** backlog

7 We don't make any profit on it. We're using it as a _____ to get market share.
   a) trademark   **b)** loss-leader   **c)** concession

8 We're paying _____ of about six per cent on our finance.
   a) tax   **b)** penalties   **c)** interest

9 We're moving our headquarters to a new _____ next month.
   a) leasehold   **b)** location   **c)** construction

10 Everyone agreed so it was a _____ decision.
   a) unanimous   **b)** summary   **c)** representative

11 I hope the terms of the agreement are to your _____ .
   a) satisfaction   **b)** entertainment   **c)** convenience

12 Don't forget to put _____ at the end of the agenda.
   a) SAE   **b)** AOB   **c)** CEO

13 Tell the _____ we need to assess the damage before we can pay anything.
   a) end user   **b)** broker   **c)** claimant

14 They're going to streamline the management _____ to reduce costs.
   a) administration   **b)** orientation   **c)** structure

15 I think the brand's strong enough to _____ into financial services.
   a) diversify   **b)** globalise   **c)** innovate

16 We're going to start _____ our computer systems in autumn.
   a) renovating   **b)** upgrading   **c)** constructing

17 The new product features should give us a competitive _____ .
   a) expectancy   **b)** premium   **c)** advantage

18 We improved our _____ channels to get products into shops more quickly.
   a) distribution   **b)** consignment   **c)** transaction

19 We'll have to be very careful how we _____ such a small budget.
   a) supervise   **b)** allocate   **c)** finance

20 The company went bankrupt and called in the _____ .
   a) auditors   **b)** accountants   **c)** receivers

21 A major social media campaign should help to increase brand _____ .
   a) feedback   **b)** reputation   **c)** awareness

22 The contractor put in a _____ for the construction project.
   a) grant   **b)** statement   **c)** tender

23 We put our savings into a high-interest _____ account.
   a) deposit   **b)** deficit   **c)** debit

24 We work very hard at _____ good relationships with our customers.
   a) launching   **b)** establishing   **c)** negotiating

25 We're hoping to pay off the _____ credit by the end of the year.
   a) pending   **b)** outstanding   **c)** overdrawn

26 The bank only invests in companies that follow strict _____ policies on child labour.
   a) ideals **b)** brand **c)** ethical

27 The motorways and new airport have improved the _____ .
   a) capacity **b)** commuting **c)** infrastructure

28 With a modest budget we had to go for the most _____ plan.
   a) cost-effective **b)** sophisticated **c)** state-of-the-art

29 They've got a good _____ of designing innovative products.
   a) analysis **b)** track record **c)** assessment

30 Some of their advertising _____ are very amusing.
   a) slogans **b)** values **c)** ethics

31 With all these new orders, we're struggling to _____ demand.
   a) produce **b)** cater **c)** satisfy

32 The trainee made a lot of mistakes due to a lack of adequate _____ .
   a) brainstorming **b)** supervision **c)** control

33 We produce locally to avoid the high import _____ .
   a) tariff **b)** bonus **c)** price

34 We use a _____ firm to distribute our heavy machinery all over the UK.
   a) haulage **b)** courier **c)** public transport

35 With _____ below two per cent, prices haven't increased for two years now.
   a) income tax **b)** depreciation **c)** inflation

36 They _____ the product due to falling sales after eight years on the market.
   a) recalled **b)** prevented **c)** discontinued

37 You have to fill in two forms to claim back your travel _____ .
   a) overheads **b)** expenses **c)** investments

38 It all depends on your _____ of view, doesn't it?
   a) point **b)** type **c)** angle

39 They took out a _____ to stop other companies copying the design.
   a) warranty **b)** patent **c)** deed

40 The _____ investment in the new factory caused financial problems.
   a) sensible **b)** suitable **c)** substantial

41 Many _____ dotcom companies go bankrupt within 18 months.
   a) established **b)** start-up **c)** preliminary

42 I have to report to my _____ every two weeks.
   a) chief executive **b)** executive assistant **c)** line manager

43 All 230 _____ stayed in the same hotel where the conference was held.
   a) members **b)** delegates **c)** guests

44 My _____ takes care of all my correspondence and my diary.
   a) partner **b)** apprentice **c)** assistant

45 Many UK supermarkets have _____ their brands into banking services.
   a) pushed **b)** diverted **c)** stretched

46 Companies need to _____ their Ethical Engagement Policies or the bank won't invest in them.
   a) comply with **b)** appeal to **c)** bring about

47 Make sure the goods are all in order before you sign the _____ note.
   a) advice **b)** cover **c)** delivery

48 We have to submit our tax _____ to the tax office by 8 February.
   a) remittance **b)** return **c)** application

49 If sales don't pick up, we'll have to review our pricing _____ .
   a) policy **b)** prediction **c)** value

50 We need to freshen up the window displays at our retail _____ .
   a) offices **b)** outlets **c)** facilities.

Reporting

Adjectives and adverbs

Form   **Adjectives and adverbs have the following forms.**

sudden	*(+ **ly**)*	*suddenly*
steady	*(~~y~~ + **ily**)*	*steadily*
dramatic	*(-ic + **ally**)*	*dramatically*
monthly	*(ly = **no change**)*	*monthly*

Use   **Adjectives are used in the following ways.**

- before nouns
  *The UK only recycles a **small** amount of municipal waste.*

- after the verbs *be, become, seem, appear, look, feel, remain*
  *The valuation seemed **low** for a company of that size.*

Adverbs are used in the following ways.

- after verbs
  *Operating profit increased **slowly** during the year.*

- before adjectives
  *Landfill space is becoming **increasingly** expensive.*

- before other adverbs
  *The industry was hit **extremely** badly by the recession.*

Note!   **Some adverbs have irregular forms.**

good – well   *fast – fast*   *late – late*   *hard – hard*

Relative clauses

Form   **Relative clauses can be defining or non-defining and use these pronouns.**

that   *who*   *which*   *whose*

Defining clauses define a noun and have the following forms.

- with *who, which* or *that* (no commas)
  *They've adjusted the forecasts **which / that** they made six months ago.*

- without a pronoun (if it is the object of the verb in the clause)
  *We've started the expansion programme **(that)** we announced in July.*

- with *whose* (to show possession)
  *That's the company **whose** shares were floated on the stock market.*

Non-defining clauses give extra information and have the following forms.

- with *who, which* or *whose* (extra information separated by commas)
  *The figures, **which** were released yesterday, caused a 10% rise in shares.*
  *The company, **whose** CEO is Swedish, is located in the Ukraine.*

Note!   ***That* is used only in defining relative clauses.**

The report, ~~that~~ was published yesterday, shocked its readers.
*The report, **which** was published yesterday, shocked its readers.*

Grammar practice

Adjectives and adverbs

1 **Complete the report with the correct form of the words in brackets.**

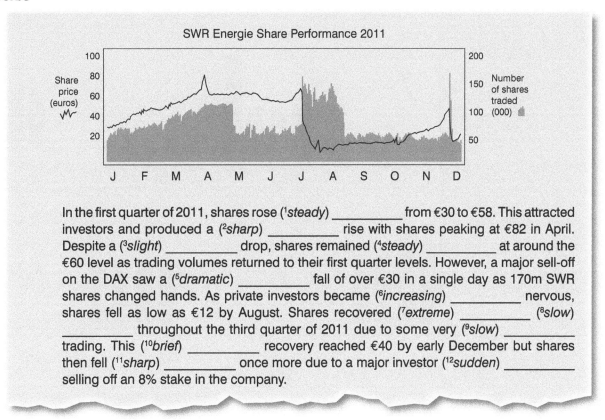

In the first quarter of 2011, shares rose (¹*steady*) _____ from €30 to €58. This attracted investors and produced a (²*sharp*) _____ rise with shares peaking at €82 in April. Despite a (³*slight*) _____ drop, shares remained (⁴*steady*) _____ at around the €60 level as trading volumes returned to their first quarter levels. However, a major sell-off on the DAX saw a (⁵*dramatic*) _____ fall of over €30 in a single day as 170m SWR shares changed hands. As private investors became (⁶*increasing*) _____ nervous, shares fell as low as €12 by August. Shares recovered (⁷*extreme*) _____ (⁸*slow*) _____ throughout the third quarter of 2011 due to some very (⁹*slow*) _____ trading. This (¹⁰*brief*) _____ recovery reached €40 by early December but shares then fell (¹¹*sharp*) _____ once more due to a major investor (¹²*sudden*) _____ selling off an 8% stake in the company.

Relative clauses

2 **Match the sentence halves.**

1 We've just paid off the money that	**a)** upset a lot of shareholders.
2 There was an economic recession, which	**b)** we borrowed from the bank in May.
3 We've got $15m of surplus stock, which	**c)** shares have performed well all year.
4 We didn't pay a dividend this year, which	**d)** caused their shares to rise by 12%.
5 They announced a $2.2bn profit, which	**e)** badly affected our domestic sales.
6 They recruited a new CEO, who	**f)** is just sitting in our warehouse.
7 I invested in a company whose	**g)** is the end of the financial year.
8 The report's due in April, which	**h)** used to work for a main competitor.

3 **Rewrite the sentences using relative clauses.**

1 Many internet companies started last year. They are now out of business.
   Many internet companies that started last year are now out of business.

2 They wrote off $400,000 of bad debts. They couldn't recover these debts.
   _____

3 Michael O'Leary is the CEO of Ryanair. Ryanair is a low-cost airline.
   _____

4 Nick Leeson was a trader. His dealings put Barings Bank out of business.
   _____

5 The figures didn't include tax. The tax makes a big difference.
   _____

Vocabulary practice

Change **1 Match the following verbs of change with the diagrams below.**

recover   collapse   shoot up   fluctuate   reach a target   peak   halve   remain steady

1) _____   2) _____   3) _____   4) _____

5) _____   6) _____   7) _____   8) _____

2 Match the adverbs with the verbs.

	peak	fluctuate	rise	collapse	improve	fall
sharply		✓				
steadily						
slightly						

3 Complete the web page with the correct prepositions.

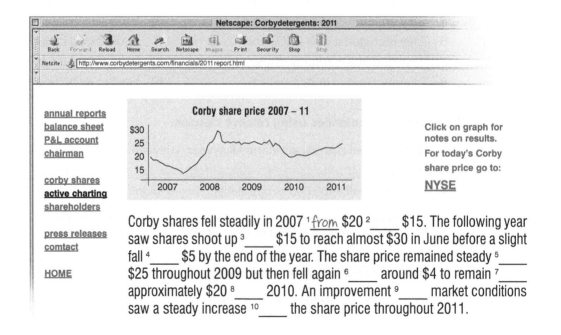

Corby shares fell steadily in 2007 [1] _from_ $20 [2] ____ $15. The following year saw shares shoot up [3] ____ $15 to reach almost $30 in June before a slight fall [4] ____ $5 by the end of the year. The share price remained steady [5] ____ $25 throughout 2009 but then fell again [6] ____ around $4 to remain [7] ____ approximately $20 [8] ____ 2010. An improvement [9] ____ market conditions saw a steady increase [10] ____ the share price throughout 2011.

4 Match the words with a similar meaning.

1	deficit	**a)**	shoot up
2	liquidation	**b)**	loss
3	soar	**c)**	devaluation
4	stock	**d)**	bankruptcy
5	surplus	**e)**	quantity
6	slump	**f)**	inventory
7	depreciation	**g)**	excess
8	volume	**h)**	recession

5 Match the words with the definitions.

1	capital assets	**a)**	people who owe money to the company
2	financial year	**b)**	all the wealth owned by a company
3	loans	**c)**	money paid to shareholders each year
4	corporation tax	**d)**	the devaluation of assets
5	creditors	**e)**	money lent to the company by a bank
6	current assets	**f)**	people the company owes money to (e.g. banks)
7	depreciation	**g)**	percentage of profits paid to the government
8	dividend	**h)**	assets that can easily be turned into cash (e.g. stock)
9	debtors	**i)**	period over which the company reports its performance

6 Your company is considering buying shares in Stanton, Inc. Write a 120–140 word report, including a recommendation of what your company should do using the following notes.

STANTON, INC.

Balance Sheet at 31 December 2011

	2010 ($000)	2011 ($000)
FIXED ASSETS		
Buildings and equipment	846	1040
Investments	200	220
	1046	1260
CURRENT ASSETS		
Stock	400	650
Debtors	450	660
Cash at bank	833	478
	1683	1788
ASSETS	2729	3048
LIABILITIES		
Loans	1460	1820
Trade creditors	200	294
Taxation	1088	1300
Dividend payable	60	120
	2808	3534
Net Assets / Liabilities	(79)	(486)

increase in unsold stock – products unpopular?

increase in debtors – customers not paying?

increase in creditors – cash flow problems?

large increase in overall debt

The workplace

Modal verbs

Use   **Modal verbs are used in the following ways.**

- to express intentions (*will, might, could* – also *going to*)
  *We **won't announce** any redundancies until next year.*
  *We **might** / **'re going to set up** a workers' council.*

- to express permission (*may, can, could* – also *allowed to*)
  ***May** / **Can** / **Could I have** a day off next week?*
  *They**'re not allowed to use** social network sites in the office.*

- to express ability (*can, could* – also *able to*)
  *The injured worker **couldn't** / **was unable to prove** company liability.*

- to make spontaneous offers (*will, can, shall*)
  ***We'll review** staffing levels if you can't cover holidays.*
  ***Can** / **Shall I get** back to you on that?*

- to make suggestions (*should, could, shall*)
  *We **should** / **could** increase the overtime bonus.*
  ***Shall** we **offer** staff two weeks' paternity leave?*

- to make requests (*can, could, would, may*)
  ***Can** / **Could** / **Would** you **inform** the shift managers, please?*
  ***May I have** a word with you?*

- to express different levels of possibility
  *They **will** / **must take** action if this absenteeism continues.* (certainty)
  *New management **should** / **would make** a difference.* (probability)
  *They **may** / **might** / **can** / **could sue** us for unfair dismissal.* (possibility)

- to express obligation (*must, should* – also *have to*)
  *All foreign workers **must** / **should** / **have to have** a work permit.*

Passive

Form   **The passive has the following forms.**

subject + correct tense of the verb *be* + past participle
*The code of practice **is updated** every year.*
*The company **was sued** for unfair dismissal.*
*One of the managers **has been suspended** on full pay.*
*Paternity leave **won't be offered** until next year.*
*Where **is** the tribunal **being held**?*

Use   **The passive is used in the following ways.**

- when the agent is unimportant or unknown
  *The minimum wage **has been increased** by four per cent.*

- to describe systems and processes
  *All disciplinary hearings **are conducted** by a committee.*

- to create an impersonal or formal style
  *I am delighted to inform you that damages of $22,000 **have been awarded**.*

Grammar practice

Modal verbs **1 Choose the correct word or phrase to complete the sentences.**

1 He cut his hand on a machine. I think he *might*/*can* need some stitches.
2 Employees *don't have to*/*mustn't* use social networking sites.
3 *May*/*Would* I use your phone, please?
4 I think you *shall*/*should* get some legal advice.
5 Don't worry, I *'ll*/*should* tell Karen that you're not coming in today.
6 Men *can*/*must* take two weeks' paternity leave after the birth of a child.
7 A good risk assessment *can*/*shall* prevent most accidents from happening.
8 We don't know if it's OK. We *'ll have*/*'re allowed* to ask the inspector when he arrives.

2 Which is the odd verb out? What uses of modal verbs do the other examples show?

1	I'm going to	(I should)	I might	I'll	*intentions*
2	She may	She's allowed to	She can	She might	_____
3	I must	I can	I'm able to	I could	_____
4	He'll	He's allowed to	He could	He might	_____
5	They mustn't	They shouldn't	They don't have to	They can't	_____
6	May I	Will I	Can I	Could I	_____
7	We should	Shall we	We could	We will	_____
8	Shall I	I may	I'll	Can I	_____

Passive **3 Complete the accident report with the correct passive or active forms.**

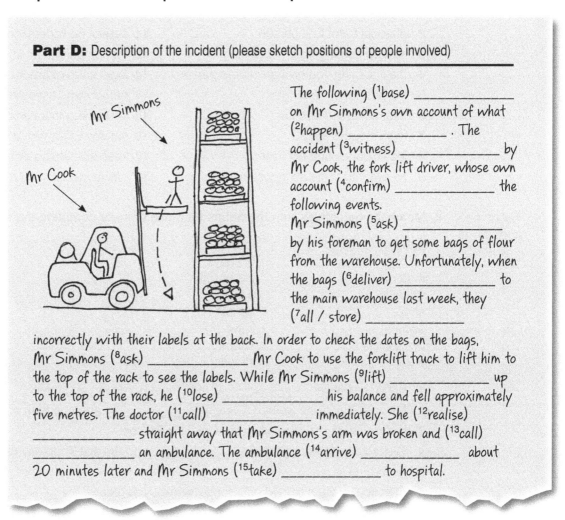

Part D: Description of the incident (please sketch positions of people involved)

Mr Simmons

Mr Cook

The following (¹base) _____ on Mr Simmons's own account of what (²happen) _____ . The accident (³witness) _____ by Mr Cook, the fork lift driver, whose own account (⁴confirm) _____ the following events.
Mr Simmons (⁵ask) _____ by his foreman to get some bags of flour from the warehouse. Unfortunately, when the bags (⁶deliver) _____ to the main warehouse last week, they (⁷all / store) _____ incorrectly with their labels at the back. In order to check the dates on the bags, Mr Simmons (⁸ask) _____ Mr Cook to use the forklift truck to lift him to the top of the rack to see the labels. While Mr Simmons (⁹lift) _____ up to the top of the rack, he (¹⁰lose) _____ his balance and fell approximately five metres. The doctor (¹¹call) _____ immediately. She (¹²realise) _____ straight away that Mr Simmons's arm was broken and (¹³call) _____ an ambulance. The ambulance (¹⁴arrive) _____ about 20 minutes later and Mr Simmons (¹⁵take) _____ to hospital.

Vocabulary

Health and safety

1 Use the clues below to find the 18 health and safety words in the puzzle.

A	T	A	C	C	I	D	E	N	T	I	I
P	R	E	V	E	N	T	W	A	I	N	N
A	I	I	F	R	J	J	M	T	L	H	S
S	B	S	S	I	U	C	S	R	I	A	P
S	U	D	L	K	R	A	T	I	A	Z	E
E	N	O	A	E	Y	S	I	P	B	A	C
S	A	P	W	M	T	E	T	S	I	R	T
S	L	L	U	G	A	R	C	A	L	D	O
M	R	U	L	I	N	G	H	O	I	I	R
E	E	Y	P	R	O	T	E	C	T	D	P
N	F	O	D	U	R	U	S	S	Y	E	A
T	P	R	E	C	A	U	T	I	O	N	S

1 an event where someone is hurt
2 physical harm to a person
3 stop something from happening
4 the first thing you give an injured person
5 the possibility of danger
6 treatment for a bad cut
7 legal responsibility
8 lose balance and fall over
9 an event to settle an industrial dispute
10 a matter being officially investigated
11 careful consideration of danger
12 money paid to an injured person
13 legal code of practice
14 person who assesses danger or risk
15 something that can cause danger
16 actions to prevent accidents
17 keep something safe from harm
18 official decision by a judge

Terms and conditions

2 Match the adjectives with the nouns then use them to complete the sentences below.

public	rate
hourly	holidays
maternity	procedure
sickness	packet
shop	benefit
social	leave
disciplinary	steward
wage	security

1 Britain has fewer _public holidays_ than most European countries.
2 My company gives women a year's _____ after the birth of a child.
3 If you want to join the union, see Craig McTeir, the _____ .
4 Our factory workers get their _____ on the last Thursday of the month.
5 According to our _____ you get a spoken warning before a written one.
6 After you've been signed off ill for six weeks, you receive the _____ .
7 I get a salary so I don't have an _____ and I don't get paid overtime.
8 I didn't get any redundancy money so I have to live off _____ .

Disciplinary procedure

3 **Use the following words and phrases to complete the dialogue below.**

> unfair dismissal   notify   absent   time off   rights   sue
> time-keeping   ultimatum   disciplinary   suspended

Joe   Hi Milly. Have you heard the news?
Milly   No, what's happened?
Joe   They've sacked Colin.
Milly   No! I thought he'd be [1] _____suspended_____ or something, but not sacked.
Joe   Well, he has got a terrible [2] _____ record. He's always in trouble.
Milly   I know he's had a lot of [3] _____ recently but ...
Joe   He's [4] _____ more often than he's here. And even when he does come to work, his [5] _____ is bad. He arrives late and leaves early.
Milly   How did he take it?
Joe   Well, he told Aziza he's going to [6] _____ the company.
Milly   You're joking! I suppose if anybody knows their [7] _____ and all about employment law, it's Colin.
Joe   I don't see how he can win an [8] _____ case, though. Not with his record. Anyway he said he's going to [9] _____ his lawyer and she'll take the appropriate action unless they give him his job back in two days.
Milly   No! He's given the company an [10] _____ ! I would have loved to have seen Aziza's face when he said that.
Joe   Actually I think she's quite pleased to finally get rid of him.

In court

4 **Match the people with the definitions.**

1 attorney   a) stands accused of breaking the law
2 plaintiff   b) prepares legal documents and represents clients
3 prosecutor   c) has the authority to decide court cases
4 defendant   d) gives evidence in court
5 juror   e) takes legal action against someone
6 judge   f) decides whether a defendant is guilty
7 witness   g) brings charges against someone in court

Word formation

5 **Complete the table then use the words to complete the sentences below.**

adjective	noun
redundant	_redundancy_
absent	_____
_____	fraud
liable	_____
_____	exemption
suspended	_____

1 The managers received generous __redundancy__ settlements after losing their jobs.
2 Production was affected by the _____ of several workers who were ill.
3 She was given a warning after making several _____ expenses claims.
4 The company refused to admit _____ for the accident.
5 As a result of the UK government not signing the European Workers' Charter, UK companies are _____ from certain EU employment laws.
6 A _____ employee is not allowed on company premises before receiving notification from the company.

Business travel

Indirect questions

Form   **Indirect questions have the following forms.**

Yes /no questions (using *if /whether*)
*Could you tell me **if /whether there is** a train to Geneva?*

Wh-questions
*Could you tell me **when** the Prague flight **is boarding**, please?*

The subject and verb are not inverted. The auxiliary verb *do* is not used.
*Could you tell me **when the plane leaves**?*
*Could you tell me **when he left** for the airport?*

Use   **Indirect questions are used in the following way.**

- to ask questions in a polite or indirect way
  *Could you tell me **how much** the room costs?*

Reported speech

Form   **Verbs used to report speech can be followed by**

- the tense used by the speaker
  *She **said** (that) the hotel **is** completely full.*

- a tense change (*admit, argue, complain, explain, promise, say*)
  *She **said** (that) the hotel **was** completely full.*

- an infinitive (*agree, ask, decide, demand, expect, offer, promise, refuse, want*)
  *He **refused to let** me take my case on board as hand luggage.*

- a gerund (*admit, deny, mention, report*)
  *She **denied booking** an expensive hotel on purpose.*

- an object + infinitive (*advise, ask, expect, instruct, invite, remind, tell, warn*)
  *He **reminded me to confirm** my return flight 24 hours in advance.*

Note!   **Note the following tense and time changes.**

*'**I'm doing** it **now**.'*	*She said (that) she **was doing** it **then**.*
*'We **did** it **yesterday**.'*	*They said (that) they **had done** it **the day before**.*
*'I **was** there a year **ago**.'*	*He said (that) he**'d been** there a year **before**.*
*'I**'ve been** to Buenos Aires.'*	*She said (that) he**'d been** to Buenos Aires.*
*'We**'ll send** them **this** week.'*	*They said (that) they**'d send** them **that** week.*
*'They**'re arriving tomorrow**.'*	*They said (that) they **were arriving the next day**.*

Verbs of suggesting

Form   **The verbs *suggest, recommend* and *advise* are never followed immediately by *to*. They are often followed by *-ing* or *that*.**

I suggest ~~to book~~ your ticket early.
I suggest booking your ticket early.
I suggest (that) you book your ticket early.

Grammar practice

Indirect
questions **1 Rewrite the questions as indirect questions.**

1 'What gate number is it?'
Could you tell me _____

2 'Where is the check-in desk?'
Could you tell me _____

3 'Do you have any foreign currency?'
Could you tell me _____

4 'Did you get any frequent-flyer miles?'
Could you tell me _____

5 'When did you leave?'
Could you tell me _____

6 'Have they reimbursed your expenses?'
Could you tell me _____

7 'Why is there a delay?'
Could you tell me _____

8 'How does this seat recline?'
Could you tell me _____

Reporting
verbs **2 Rewrite the statements using the following reporting verbs.**

complain	invite	warn	explain	suggest
remind	offer	recommend	refuse	deny

1 'I'm sorry for the delay but the inbound flight arrived late.'
The flight attendant *explained that the inbound flight had arrived late.*

2 'It's just not good enough! We've been waiting here for over three hours now.'
The man _____

3 'You should try to get an upgrade'
The woman _____

4 'Don't forget to take your passport.'
She _____

5 'No, I won't book the hotel room for you. Do it yourself.'
He _____

6 'I could phone the hotel and book a room for you.'
The travel agent _____

7 'Don't go out on your own at night in the city.'
The hotel receptionist _____

8 'I'd stay at the Park Plaza if I were you. It's an excellent hotel.'
The travel agent _____

9 'Of course I didn't change any information on my expenses form.'
He _____

10 You'll have to come and stay with us for a weekend some time.'
They _____

3 Which reporting verb is the odd one out? What follows the other verbs?

1	expect	invite	warn	(complain)	*object + infinitive*
2	say	refuse	admit	argue	_____
3	want	offer	explain	demand	_____
4	deny	remind	mention	report	_____

Vocabulary practice

1 Match the words then use them to complete the sentences.

baggage	lounge
connecting	allowance
frequent	gate
departure	baggage
onboard	flight
boarding	currency
excess	entertainment
foreign	flyer

1 All those brochures in your bag are going to weigh more than the _baggage allowance_ .

2 Once we land at JFK, we have 30 minutes to catch our _____ to Denver.

3 The _____ was excellent. I watched two films and a documentary.

4 Please wait in the _____ and the gate number will be announced shortly.

5 As a _____ , I earn lots of airmiles which I use to go on holiday with.

6 Could passengers for BA576 please proceed to _____ 44A.

7 Excuse me. Can you use _____ when buying duty free on board?

8 I took all those books with me and had to pay for _____ when I checked in.

2 Use the following words to complete the web page below.

allocation	refunds	online	cancellation
transferred	refreshments	check-in	proof

Netscape: a2z.com/flights

Back Forward Reload Home Search Netscape Images Print Security Shop Stop

Netsite: http://www.a2z.com/flights/bookings/terms.htm

terms & conditions

home   help   destinations   flights   online security

▶ BOOK NOW

terms & conditions

Prices include air fare, airport tax and light ¹_____ (hot drink and a biscuit) served on European flights. As an ²_____ booking service, we do not issue tickets. Print out your flight confirmation details as ³_____ of purchase. These should be presented at ⁴_____ . Note there is no seat ⁵_____ and passengers can use any available seat on the plane. In the case of ⁶_____ of a flight, passengers will be ⁷_____ to the next available flight. We are unable to offer ⁸_____ in the case of a passenger having to cancel a confirmed seat reservation.

3 Which word is the odd one out?

1 itinerary	claim	schedule	programme
2 notify	inform	authorise	announce
3 check-in	embark	board	get on
4 catering	refreshments	entertainment	snack
5 deal with	process	handle	delegate
6 scheduled	connecting	charter	package

4 **Write the words in the correct groups then complete the sentences.**

| add | minus | times | plus | deduct |
| comes to | | multiply | equals | divide |

+	−	x	÷	=

1 Four _____ twelve _____ sixteen.
2 If you _____ six from twenty-four, you get eighteen.
3 When you _____ seven by seven, you get forty-nine.
4 If you _____ thirty-six and twenty-seven, you get sixty-three.
5 If you _____ £1,800 by 2.61, you get £689.66.
6 Twenty-two _____ five is a hundred and ten.
7 _____ 10% VAT to $326 and you get $358.60.
8 So that's €1,628, _____ €360 discount, which is €1,268.

5 **Match the verbs with the nouns and then use them to complete the sentences.**

submit ———————— a system
scan ——————————— a claim
log in to   a claim
implement   an account
reimburse   receipts
process   expenses

1 With expenses, you need to _submit claims_ online now.
2 Please _____ and attach them to the online claim form.
3 We normally _____ as part of an employee's next monthly salary.
4 The company is _____ a new _____ for claiming expenses.
5 The new system will cut the cost of _____ and speed things up.
6 Each employee will have a password to _____ their own expenses _____ .

6 **You have been asked to prepare an itinerary for a Mrs Gudjohnson, who is visiting your company in Frankfurt. Use your handwritten notes below to write a formal letter to Mrs Gudjohnson confirming the details of her trip. Write 120–140 words.**

Gudjohnson trip 24–26 May
Thursday 24: arrive Frankfurt 10:40 (don't
forget to book taxi to meet her)
11:30 – show her round the company
12:30 – lunch (with Mirijana Kurtz)
3.00 – visit SKA GmbH in Wiesbaden
Should be back at her hotel by 5 pm
20.00 – dinner at hotel with Pierre
Bonner

Friday 25
9.00 – visit Kahn & Sohn (supplier)
13.00 – lunch in Frankfurt
2.30 – meeting with MD Michael
Thomas & Sales Director Suzanna
Köpke until about 5.00.

Remember – confirm return
flight for Saturday 26 May
8.40am Copenhagen!

People

Gerunds (-ing forms)

Form   **Gerunds are used in the following ways.**

- as nouns
  *We've been trying to do a lot more **training**.*

- after prepositions
  *We won't offer anyone a job **without checking** their references.*

- after certain verbs (see the list below)
  *I'd like to **avoid commuting** to work if I can.*
  *We can't **continue not replacing** staff that leave the company.*

Here are some verbs often followed by a gerund.

admit	delay	go	mention	recommend
attempt	deny	hate	mind	report
avoid	dislike	imagine	miss	risk
begin	enjoy	keep	prefer	start
celebrate	face	like	postpone	suggest
continue	finish	love	practise	

Infinitives

Form   **Infinitives have the following forms.**

*We **hope to find** someone for the job next month.*
*She **chose not to stay** at the Plaza Hotel.*
*They **wouldn't negotiate** new salaries.* (no *to* after modal verbs)

Use   **Infinitives are used in the following ways.**

- after certain verbs (see the list below)
  *I **managed to get** a room at the last minute.*

- after adjectives (often with *too* or *enough*)
  *It's **important to have** in-room communication facilities.*

These verbs are often followed by an infinitive.

afford	demand	plan	ask (someone to ...)
agree	hope	prepare	expect (someone to ...)
appear	intend	promise	invite (someone to ...)
arrange	manage	refuse	remind (someone to ...)
choose	need	seem	tell (someone to ...)
decide	offer	want	warn (someone to ...)

Note!   **Some verbs can be followed by either a gerund or an infinitive.**

- with no difference (*begin, hate, like, love, prefer, start*)
  *We **prefer promoting** /**to promote** our own staff.*

- with a time difference (*forget, remember, regret*)
  *Do you **remember working** in the old building.* (refers to the past)
  ***Remember to post** that letter, won't you?* (refers to the present/future)

Grammar practice

Gerunds **1 Match the sentence halves.**

1 I emailed my application. I didn't risk
2 I enjoy business travel. I like
3 I took a taxi. I couldn't face
4 I went to Paris for two days to celebrate
5 We shortlist candidates once we finish
6 My girlfriend helped me practise
7 We decided to delay
8 I started

a) getting the new job.
b) sending it by post.
c) travelling on the underground.
d) visiting new and different countries.
e) advertising the post until she'd left.
f) answering interview-type questions.
g) learning Spanish eight months ago.
h) interviewing all the applicants.

Gerunds and infinitives **2 Complete the conversation with the correct form of the verbs in brackets.**

Maureen	So, Dexter, we've finally managed (¹*find*) _____ time for your appraisal. I'm sorry I've been so slow (²*get*) _____ round to it.
Dexter	That's OK. Everyone seems (³*be*) _____ so busy right now.
Maureen	Yes, they do. It's that time of year again, isn't it? Anyway, we're here now. Did you remember (⁴*bring*) _____ your appraisal form?
Dexter	Here it is.
Maureen	Did you have any difficulties in (⁵*fill*) _____ it in?
Dexter	Not really, though I must admit (⁶*not/be*) _____ too sure about one or two bits of it.
Maureen	That's OK. Should we just start (⁷*work*) _____ our way through it from the beginning and see how it goes?
Dexter	Yeah. Sure.
Maureen	So, the first thing is what you've been doing over the last twelve months. So what do we have here ...
Dexter	Well, as you can see, it's mainly been the Service2012 research project.
Maureen	Oh yes. And how's it going?
Dexter	Fine. I don't want (⁸*sound*) _____ too confident, but we should (⁹*manage*) _____ (¹⁰*meet*) _____ next month's deadline without too much difficulty.
Maureen	Well, that's good. Well done. And was it difficult (¹¹*get*) _____ all the information together that you needed?
Dexter	We've been very lucky (¹²*not/have*) _____ had any problems. All the regional offices have been really helpful and co-operative. It would've been a lot harder (¹³*get*) _____ all the data we needed if they hadn't been so helpful. There were one or two offices that we had to keep (¹⁴*ask*) _____ for information, but on the whole everyone was very co-operative.
Maureen	That's great. And what was it like working with the rest of the team?
Dexter	Fine. They're all really easy (¹⁵*get*) _____ on with. I've enjoyed (¹⁶*work*) _____ with them. (¹⁷*meet*) _____ colleagues from other offices has been very interesting. You find out all sorts of things about the company.
Maureen	I bet you do.
Dexter	I quite enjoyed (¹⁸*travel*) _____ around the country a bit and (¹⁹*visit*) _____ the other offices too. I think I'll quite miss (²⁰*work*) _____ on the Service2012 team when the project comes to an end next month.
Maureen	In terms of development, what do you think you've learnt from ...

Vocabulary practice

Appraisals **1 Complete the word diagram with the following appraisal words.**

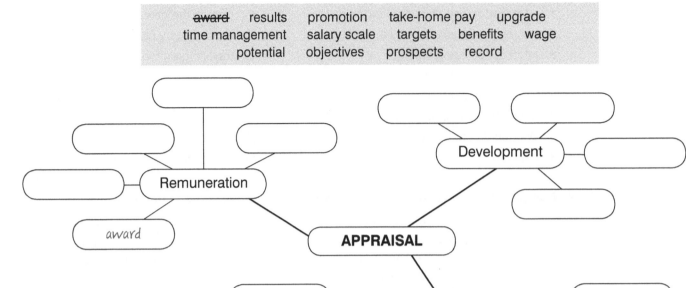

~~award~~   results   promotion   take-home pay   upgrade
time management   salary scale   targets   benefits   wage
potential   objectives   prospects   record

Remuneration

award

Development

APPRAISAL

Performance

Word formation **2 Complete the table then use the words to complete the sentences below.**

verb	noun
appraise	*appraisal*
	criticism
notify	_____
assign	_____
	approval
develop	_____
permit	_____
	remuneration
evaluate	_____

1 I've got my performance __*appraisal*__ next month with my line manager.
2 The promotion takes immediate effect but you won't get the official letter of _____ until some time next month.
3 Our _____ committee is reviewing all salary scales at the moment.
4 It's often very difficult to _____ performance in customer service.
5 We don't just look at past performance. We also discuss your future _____ .
6 It's not just negative _____ . We're trying to point out areas where you could perform better.
7 I'm afraid company rules don't _____ people to be promoted up two grades of management in the same year.
8 The Managing Director has to _____ all promotions before they're made.
9 We're going to _____ you to a special projects team which will be taking a close look at our budgets over the next few months.

Trade unions **3 Match the words with the definitions.**

1	bargaining power	a)	disagreement
2	blue-collar worker	b)	negotiating strength
3	closed shop	c)	organised refusal to work
4	dispute	d)	person who works in an office
5	industrial relations	e)	when all employees must be union members
6	mediation	f)	person who works on the factory floor
7	white-collar worker	g)	dealings between employers and employees
8	strike	h)	using a neutral person to solve a disagreement

Personnel **4 Which word does not go with the word in capital letters?**

1 WORKER
unskilled   blue-collar   retirement   temporary

2 JOB
satisfaction   testimonial   security   description

3 SELECTION
procedure   council   committee   process

4 WORK
force   permit   schedule   aptitude

5 PAY
shift   packet   roll   slip

6 PERSONNEL
officer   management   development   vacation

7 LEAVE
maternity   annual   redundancy   paid

8 STAFF
quantity   turnover   shortage   levels

Recruitment **5 Use the clues below to complete the puzzle.**

temp   basic wage   references   advertise   headhunt   rank   shortlist

1 level of seniority of a job title
2 person employed for a short period of time only – often holiday cover
3 amount of remuneration before bonuses and benefits
4 companies usually check these before offering a job
5 way of recruiting people who work for other companies
6 show a vacancy in a newspaper or on the internet
7 reduce the number of candidates after a first round of interviews

Marketing

Conditional 1 (real)

Form **Conditionals expressing real possibility have the following forms.**

if + present tense, present tense
*If products **don't sell** well, we **drop** the price to create demand.*

if + present tense, modal verb + infinitive
*If we **license** production, we**'ll cut** production costs.*
*We **might lose** some goodwill if we **change** to a hard-sell strategy.*

Use **These conditionals are used in the following ways.**

- to show cause and effect
  *If we **increase** the price, the volume of sales **drops**.*
- to predict the effect of an action
  *It's **going to increase** profitability if we **target** our top 70% of customers.*
- to request action if something happens
  ***Review** the pricing policy if sales **don't pick up** next month.*

Note! **If introduces a possible event. When introduces a definite event.**

*Increase the price **if** sales go up.* (Sales might go up.)
*Let me know **when** the brochures arrive.* (The brochures will definitely arrive.)

Conditional 2 (hypothetical)

Form **Conditionals expressing hypothetical situations have the following forms.**

hypothetical situations in the present or future

if + past tense, *would* / *could* / *might* + infinitive
*If we **brought** the launch forward to next week, we**'d get** more press coverage.*
*Customers **might be** interested in package deals if the prices **were** attractive.*

hypothetical situations in the past

if + had + past participle, *would* / *could* / *might* + have + past participle
*If we**'d released** the product earlier, we **would have sold** a lot more.*
*We **could** / **might have made** more impact if we**'d had** a bigger budget.*

The hypothetical present and future form of be is always were.

*I wouldn't launch the new product yet if I **were** you.*

Use **Hypothetical conditionals are used in the following ways.**

- to talk about hypothetical situations
  *If we **cut** prices, we**'d lose** money.* (= we're unlikely to cut prices)
  *We **would have changed** the name if we**'d known**.* (= we didn't know)
  *We**'d have produced** more if we**'d had** good forecasts.* (= forecasts were bad)

Note! **Some hypothetical conditionals can mix present and past verb forms.**

*If we **hadn't done** so much research, our products **wouldn't be** so good now.*

Grammar practice

Real possibility **1 Complete the sentences with the correct form of the verb in brackets.**

1 We'll have to increase our advertising if sales (*not/go*) _____ up soon.

2 If you display snacks near supermarket check-outs, sales (*increase*) _____ .

3 We'll do a new brochure if we (*switch*) _____ to pricing in euros.

4 If we don't target our customers better, they (*not/know*) _____ about our newest product offerings.

5 If the feedback isn't positive, we (*rethink*) _____ the packaging design.

6 There's no point in having a loss-leader if it (*not/win*) _____ market share.

7 If we (*not/find*) _____ a suitable joint-venture partner, then we'll look into the possibility of franchising agreements.

8 If a company recruits more sales executives, it usually (*sell*) _____ more products.

Hypothetical situations **2 Use the following information to write hypothetical sentences.**

1 our products don't sell well / they are too expensive.
   Our products would sell better if they weren't so expensive.

2 we don't give free samples / they cost too much money
   _____

3 our website isn't very attractive / we don't have a trained graphic designer
   _____

4 we didn't go to the trade fair / we didn't see our competitor's new products
   _____

5 we can't do a mailshot / our mailing list is too small
   _____

6 the product didn't sell well / it had some bad publicity in the newspapers
   _____

7 not many customers subscribe to the website / few have heard about it
   _____

8 the TV advert was very popular / the product sold very well
   _____

9 we want the product to sell well in Germany / we need to change the name
   _____

10 we had a lot of quality problems / we didn't delay the launch by six weeks
   _____

Conditionals **3 Complete the sentences with the correct form of the verbs in brackets.**

1 I'm sure it (*sell*) _____ really well but only if we (*target*) _____ the right type of customer and (*launch*) _____ it within the next six months.

2 We (*not/be*) _____ able to get all this information about the Chinese market if Johnny (*not/make*) _____ the trip to Hong Kong last month.

3 I (*not/target*) _____ the mid-teen market if I (*be*) _____ you. They won't have the money to buy the product. I (*go*) _____ for the 18–20s.

4 It was a smart move setting up the local sales operation. They (*not/be*) _____ as successful if they (*continue*) _____ exporting direct from the US.

5 I'm sure we (*boost*) _____ sales if we (*redesign*) _____ all our packaging, but I doubt it (*be*) _____ a good return on the investment required to do it.

6 Studies show that we (*increase*) _____ customer loyalty and brand awareness if we (*open*) _____ up our own retail outlets rather than distributing through department stores. So that's what we're going to do.

Vocabulary practice

Marketing

1 Complete the word diagram with the following marketing words.

subscription   free sample   flood   exhibition   outlets   dominate
sponsorship   chain stores   media   saturate   boom   franchise
direct selling   word of mouth   TV adverts   break into

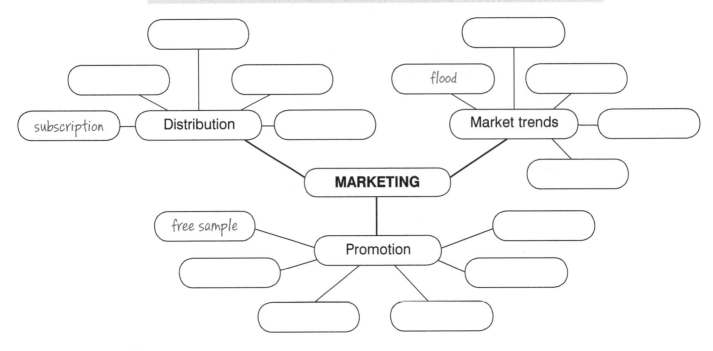

2 Match the words with the definitions.

1	positioning	a)	sell another company's goods under strict guidelines
2	mark-up	b)	placing of a product in a market (price, image etc.)
3	margin	c)	strategic combination of product, price, place and promotion
4	loss-leader	d)	something to attract attention to a product
5	franchise	e)	place where a product is actually sold
6	mailshot	f)	difference between selling price and cost of production
7	gimmick	g)	amount of profit a product makes
8	point of sale	h)	product sold without profit to gain market share
9	marketing mix	i)	generation of new business with a postal promotion

3 Which word does not go with the word in capital letters?

1	MARKETING plan	lifestyle	mix	strategy
2	A PRODUCT position	withdraw	launch	saturate
3	MARKET black	target	billboard	free
4	DIRECT marketing	mail	selling	slogan
5	PRESS prospectus	conference	release	launch
6	MARKET leader	jingle	value	share

4 Complete the table then use the words to complete the sentences below.

verb	noun
promote	_promotion_
publicise	_____
_____	launch
license	_____
_____	feedback
differentiate	_____
position	_____
_____	campaign

1 We're going to run a big press __promotion__ in three national newspapers.

2 We're trying hard to _____ our products from competitors' similar offerings.

3 They had a lot of bad _____ in the papers about the safety of the product.

4 We're launching a new TV advertising _____ next week.

5 It's vital we _____ the product properly. It has to be seen as better quality than the cheaper brands but offering the same quality as the more expensive ones.

6 We got some great _____ from the marketing questionnaires.

7 We don't want to set up an expensive overseas production facility so we're going to _____ a local manufacturer to produce the goods in the US.

8 The new product's having its official _____ on May 25 at a top New York hotel.

5 Which word is the odd one out?

1	brochure	prospectus	advertisement	(report)
2	discounted	complimentary	free	gratis
3	product	performance	price	positioning
4	jingle	slogan	packaging	tune
5	trade mark	copyright	patent	logo
6	end-user	consumer	retailer	customer
7	merchandise	franchise	goods	products
8	dominate	break into	penetrate	enter

6 You work for Dayton, Inc. Look at the marketing information and handwritten notes. Write a 120–140 word report summarising the information and recommend action.

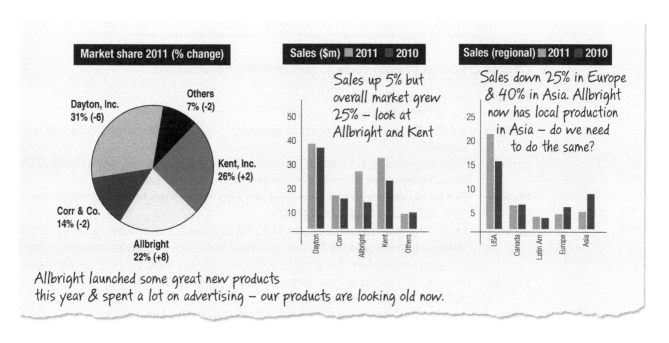

Market share 2011 (% change)

Dayton, Inc. 31% (-6)
Others 7% (-2)
Kent, Inc. 26% (+2)
Corr & Co. 14% (-2)
Allbright 22% (+8)

Sales ($m) ■ 2011 ■ 2010
Sales up 5% but overall market grew 25% – look at Allbright and Kent

Sales (regional) ■ 2011 ■ 2010
Sales down 25% in Europe & 40% in Asia. Allbright now has local production in Asia – do we need to do the same?

Allbright launched some great new products this year & spent a lot on advertising – our products are looking old now.

Review unit 2 (6–10)

Grammar

1 Rewrite the sentences using the correct form of the passive.

1 The company patented the design in 2008.
   The design was patented in 2008.

2 A local company has dominated the market for the past five years.

3 They're launching a new product in May.

4 We produce the goods under a licensing agreement.

5 We didn't organise the campaign early enough.

6 Cheap imports are saturating the market at the moment.

7 We're going to reduce our margins by 6%.

8 How did you position the product?

9 We need to differentiate the product enough from its competitor.

10 How has she marketed the new product?

11 Our customers filled in over 2,000 questionnaires.

12 Someone has written a new jingle for the TV advertisement.

13 We should have promoted the product in South America.

14 We didn't launch the product until it was absolutely reliable.

15 We give them to customers for free.

2 Choose the correct modal verbs to complete the conversation.

Philippe Hi, John. It's Philippe.
John Oh hi, Philippe. How's it going?
Philippe It's OK. But we're really short of workers. [1]*Could /Would* we take on some new people?
John That [2]*might /must* be difficult. You know we [3]*will /have* to stay within budget and you know Melanie [4]*won't /shan't* make any more money available.
Philippe But surely we [5]*shall /can* take on some agency workers for the summer? We [6]*don't have to /mustn't* take on full-timers.
John Look, I [7]*'m going to /should* see Melanie at three this afternoon, so I [8]*'ll mention / mention* it to her and we [9]*'ll see /see* what she says. I'm afraid that's all I [10]*can / could* promise. How many agency workers do you think you [11]*'ll /should* need?
Philippe [12]*Could /Will* I have at least three per shift? I don't think we [13]*may /can* manage without that many extra people.
John That's nine more. It's a lot. Melanie [14]*won't /wouldn't* like it.
Philippe I know. But see what you [15]*can /may* do.

3 Complete the sentences with a suitable relative pronoun. If the sentence does not need a pronoun, write Ø.

1 Here's the new machinery _which / that / Ø_ you ordered.
2 I don't know _____ is responsible for ordering stationery.
3 The new safety system, _____ was installed yesterday, isn't working yet.
4 _____ signature do I need to get on this form?
5 _____ did you send the report to?
6 There were a lot of safety problems _____ needed to be solved.
7 The report was written by the supervisor _____ was in charge at the time.
8 The mistakes _____ were made were mostly due to staff shortages.
9 The damaged goods were part of the order _____ arrived yesterday.
10 The figures _____ you gave me were very interesting.

4 Complete the email with the correct adjectives or adverbs.

◄ ► email	RE: Expenses report

From : Alexis Dabizas [aadabizas@sai-online.it]
Sent: Tuesday 24 July 3.01pm
To: Luisa Delvecchio
Subject: **RE: Expenses report**

Luisa

I've just about finished the report on travel expenses for the first half of the year. I'll email you the final document but here are the main findings:

- Overall, the total cost of travel expenses rose (¹*sharp*) _____ in the six months to July. This was, of course, mainly due to the recent merger, which has meant a (²*significant*) _____ increase in the amount of foreign travel undertaken by employees.

- There was a (³*slight*) _____ fall in the average expenditure per trip. This was due to (⁴*increasing*) _____ strict monitoring of expense claims and the fact that we have managed to (⁵*dramatic*) _____ reduce the number of expense claims made without receipts.

- After what seemed like (⁶*slow*) _____ progress to begin with, the cost of processing expense claims is now falling (⁷*sharp*) _____ due to the implementation of the electronic claims forms. However, many employees are still having (⁸*real*) _____ difficulties using the forms and require (⁹*urgent*) _____ training.

As I said, I hope to get the final report and (¹⁰*exact*) _____ figures to you as soon as I can – probably by the end of the week.

All the best

Alexis

5 Rewrite the following as indirect questions beginning with *Could you tell me*.

1 Excuse me. What time is it, please?
Could you tell me *what the time is, please?*

2 When is the flight for Wellington leaving?
Could you tell me _____

3 Where do I have to check in for the Paris flight?
Could you tell me _____

4 Where is check-in zone D?
Could you tell me _____

5 How long before the flight do I have to check in?
Could you tell me _____

6 Did you pack your own luggage?
Could you tell me _____

7 How many suitcases would you like to check in?
Could you tell me _____

8 Has anyone given you anything to take on board?
Could you tell me _____

9 Where can I buy a newspaper?
Could you tell me _____

10 Do you have a UK driving licence?
Could you tell me _____

6 Rewrite the sentences using reported speech.

1 'I didn't tell her to drop the price.'
He denied *telling her to drop the price* .

2 'You shouldn't take any new workers on.'
The consultant advised _____ .

3 'It's not good enough! We have to see some profits by the end of year.'
The shareholders demanded _____ .

4 'Oh, by the way, did you know Peter's getting married?'
She mentioned _____ .

5 'We're not going to cut our prices. We can't afford it.'
The Sales Manager refused _____ .

6 'Don't say anything about these latest sales figures, will you?'
My boss asked _____ .

7 'We never get enough information on company performance.'
The shareholders complained _____ .

8 'Don't worry, I'll send you the figures this week.'
She promised _____ .

9 'Market conditions have been very tough this year.'
The report explained _____ .

10 'Don't announce the figures until after the shareholders' meeting.'
He asked _____ .

7 Complete the sentences with the correct conditional forms.

Maria	So George, how have my investments been doing this year?
George	Quite well overall. They (¹*do*) _would have done_ even better if the stock market (²*not/perform*) _____ so badly.
Maria	I know. I've been worried about it all year.
George	But you haven't done too badly. If you (³*look*) _____ at the banking shares, things (⁴*look*) _____ very positive.
Maria	But what about the telecoms companies I invested in?
George	Well yes. Things (⁵*be*) _____ a lot better if we (⁶*not/invest*) _____ in those shares.
Maria	Should I sell them?
George	I (⁷*not/sell*) _____ them if I (⁸*be*) _____ you. You'll find that if you (⁹*hold on*) _____ to shares like these, they usually (¹⁰*make*) _____ a good medium to long-term investment.
Maria	And what about the technology shares? I had some of those, didn't I?
George	Only a few. Remember we decided not to risk it. It (¹¹*be*) _____ a lot worse if we (¹²*buy*) _____ a lot of them.
Maria	That's good. So what about the future?
George	Well, if I (¹³*be*) _____ you, I (¹⁴*look*) _____ to come out of risky high tech shares and think about big oil companies, for example. Something more stable.
Maria	OK. If you (¹⁵*say*) _____ so.
George	Right. That's what we'll do then.

8 Complete the email with the correct gerund or infinitive forms.

◀ ▶ email	RE: H&S inspection

From :	Stuart Howard [stuart.howard@snackworld.co.uk]
Sent:	Thursday 12 April 12.58pm
To:	Martina Stachurski
Subject:	**RE: H&S inspection**

Hi Martina

Here's an update on the main points arising from today's health and safety inspection. I've just finished (¹*speak*) _speaking_ to the inspector and I thought it would be useful (²*send*) _____ you a quick email to let you know what he said. There's no point in (³*go*) _____ into too much detail as I intend (⁴*write*) _____ a full report before the end of the week.

* Safety

  On the whole it went OK. He asked (⁵*see*) _____ the new warehouse extension even though it's too early (⁶*say*) _____ whether or not it's met safety requirements. He'll need (⁷*come*) _____ back once it's been finished. He was also very interested in (⁸*see*) _____ the staff areas.

* Hygiene

  He wasn't too impressed, I'm afraid. I admitted (⁹*not/have*) _____ had enough time to prepare for his visit and said we'd have liked to have done a bit more (¹⁰*clean*) _____ . That's not the worst bit though. Do you remember (¹¹*talk*) _____ about the problem of mice in the warehouse? Well, I regret (¹²*say*) _____ that he saw one. Typical, isn't it? Just as we began (¹³*look*) _____ around the warehouse, I saw it. I tried to stop him from (¹⁴*see*) _____ it but it was too late. He said he wouldn't mention it in his report but we need (¹⁵*solve*) _____ the problem right away.

Vocabulary

Complete each sentence with the correct option.

1 The market slowly became _____ by imitation products.
   a) targeted   b) saturated   c) merchandised

2 All expenses are _____ in the following month's pay packet.
   a) allocated   b) reimbursed   c) submitted

3 The Government has just raised the minimum hourly _____ .
   a) salary   b) bonus   c) wage

4 As part of the reorganisation we all had to rewrite our job _____ .
   a) description   b) satisfaction   c) security

5 If we don't take off soon, we'll arrive late at Frankfurt and I'll miss my _____ flight to Amsterdam.
   a) connecting   b) scheduled   c) transfer

6 They're cutting jobs due to the massive _____ in sales.
   a) slump   b) recovery   c) devaluation

7 They phoned to say I'd got the job but I haven't had a letter of _____ yet.
   a) recruitment   b) selection   c) appointment

8 That radio ad has a really nice _____, which I keep singing in my head.
   a) jingle   b) trademark   c) slogan

9 The flight was _____ due to severe weather conditions.
   a) prevented   b) notified   c) cancelled

10 Most of the company's workforce are _____ office workers.
   a) white-collar   b) apprentice   c) blue-collar

11 I was represented in court by my _____ .
   a) judge   b) shop steward   c) attorney

12 Make sure you scan all necessary _____ with your expenses claims.
   a) recipes   b) payslips   c) receipts

13 Don't forget to include two _____ at the end of your CV.
   a) references   b) evaluations   c) records

14 We prepared a _____ to send to our 2,000 top customers.
   a) mailshot   b) marketing plan   c) franchise

15 _____ assessment is about examining what could harm people at work.
   a) Security   b) Damage   c) Risk

16 My PA normally _____ all my expenses claims.
   a) deals with   b) delegates   c) incurs

17 Every year I have a performance _____ with my line manager.
   a) discussion   b) appraisal   c) testimonial

18 We need to freshen up our _____ advertising at supermarket check-outs.
   a) exhibition   b) point-of-sale   c) billboard

19 After four quarters of negative growth the country was officially in _____ .
   a) liquidation   b) recession   c) depreciation

20 We need to _____ our product more from our competitors'.
   a) differentiate   b) distribute   c) differ

21 After her dismissal she took the company to _____ .
   a) prosecution   b) law   c) court

22 The _____ won his unfair dismissal case and the company paid $20,000.
   a) plaintiff   b) defendant   c) witness

23 We ran a successful social media marketing _____ for six weeks.
   a) prospectus   b) mix   c) campaign

24 The workers went on _____ in protest against low pay.
   a) dispute   b) vacation   c) strike

25 We sold off all our _____ stock to make room in the warehouse.
   a) peak   b) inventory   c) surplus

26 The inspector said the boxes of photocopier paper were a fire _____ .
    a) hazard   **b)** precaution   **c)** liability

27 The product's losing money but it's a _____ to grow market share.
    a) gimmick   **b)** loss-leader   **c)** sample

28 After the birth of her baby she took a year's _____ leave.
    a) benefit   **b)** maternity   **c)** annual

29 The cleaner hurt her arm when she _____ on the wet floor.
    a) tripped   **b)** banged   **c)** slipped

30 Recent stock market _____ make it impossible to predict trends.
    a) excesses   **b)** fluctuations   **c)** improvements

31 The job advert mentioned an excellent _____ package.
    a) remuneration   **b)** redundancy   **c)** retirement

32 They had to _____ the product due to reliability problems.
    a) launch   **b)** withdraw   **c)** feedback

33 According to my _____, I've now got a 3.30 meeting with Mr Sorensson.
    a) inventory   **b)** strategy   **c)** schedule

34 The _____ of this appraisal is not only to review performance but also to discuss future professional development.
    a) assignment   **b)** target   **c)** objective

35 We've had problems supplying some of our retail _____ .
    a) outlets   **b)** chains   **c)** points

36 I was actually recruited by a _____, which was all very exciting.
    a) tribunal   **b)** headhunter   **c)** selection committee

37 Our website has now broken the target of 100,000 new _____ .
    a) subscriptions   **b)** purchasers   **c)** sponsorships

38 We're having problems meeting targets due to a _____ of skilled workers.
    a) short list   **b)** shortage   **c)** short term

39 Boarding will start at 4.40 at _____ 44A. Have a nice flight.
    a) gate   **b)** lounge   **c)** check-in

40 Appointing him seemed a great decision but he never fulfilled his _____ .
    a) prospects   **b)** aptitude   **c)** potential

41 As HR Manager, I have to _____ performance and decide pay rises.
    a) approve   **b)** criticise   **c)** appraise

42 The newspaper story about working conditions got us a lot of bad _____ .
    a) word of mouth   **b)** marketing   **c)** publicity

43 About 50 per cent of the employees are members of the _____ .
    a) workforce   **b)** trade union   **c)** council

44 The new online expenses system will _____ claims a lot quicker.
    a) implement   **b)** process   **c)** permit

45 There are lots of illegal imitation products available on the _____ market.
    a) free   **b)** black   **c)** direct

46 The poor conditions mean we have a high _____ of staff in our company.
    a) turnover   **b)** deficit   **c)** departure

47 Carrying all those books meant I had to pay for _____ .
    a) excess baggage   **b)** hand luggage   **c)** baggage allowance

48 The _____ in smartphone sales led to a massive increase in mobile internet usage.
    a) strength   **b)** volume   **c)** boom

49 After struggling for three years, the company finally filed for _____ .
    a) failure   **b)** bankruptcy   **c)** collapse

50 After several warnings, he was finally dismissed for poor _____ .
    a) temping   **b)** timekeeping   **c)** timing

Writing

Letters and emails

1 **A US manufacturer of musical instruments receives an enquiry from a shop in Singapore. Look at the emails and complete the table below.**

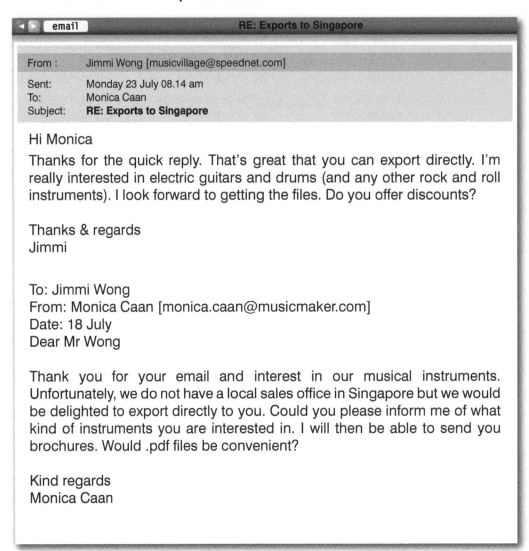

	Formal style	Informal style
opening	Dear Mr Wong	
use of contractions	No contractions e.g. thank you, we would	
vocabulary	unfortunately, delighted, inform, able to, convenient	
closing	Kind regards	

2 **Match each formal phrase on the left with a neutral phrase on the right.**

1 Thank you for your enquiry of …

2 I am delighted to hear that …

3 Unfortunately, we do not have …

4 Could you please inform me which …

5 Would it be convenient to …

6 I am able to assure you that …

7 Do not hesitate to contact me …

8 I will be able to …

a) Let me know which …

b) Thanks for your email on …

c) I can …

d) Call me …

e) I'm sorry but we don't have …

f) It's good news about …

g) I can confirm that …

h) Is it OK to …

3 **Look at the informal email. Consider the points below and rewrite the email in a more neutral / formal style.**

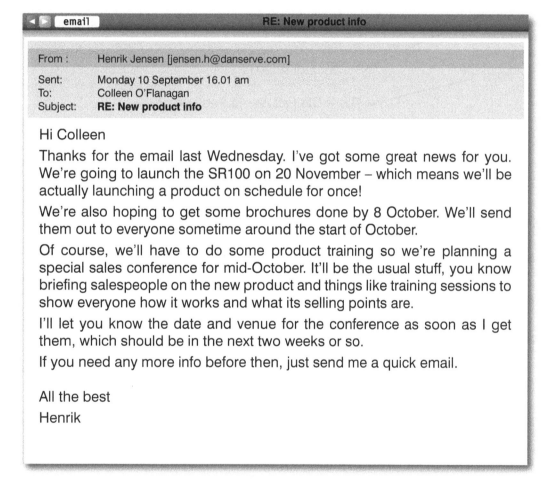

email	RE: New product info

From : Henrik Jensen [jensen.h@danserve.com]

Sent: Monday 10 September 16.01 am
To: Colleen O'Flanagan
Subject: **RE: New product info**

Hi Colleen

Thanks for the email last Wednesday. I've got some great news for you. We're going to launch the SR100 on 20 November – which means we'll be actually launching a product on schedule for once!

We're also hoping to get some brochures done by 8 October. We'll send them out to everyone sometime around the start of October.

Of course, we'll have to do some product training so we're planning a special sales conference for mid-October. It'll be the usual stuff, you know briefing salespeople on the new product and things like training sessions to show everyone how it works and what its selling points are.

I'll let you know the date and venue for the conference as soon as I get them, which should be in the next two weeks or so.

If you need any more info before then, just send me a quick email.

All the best
Henrik

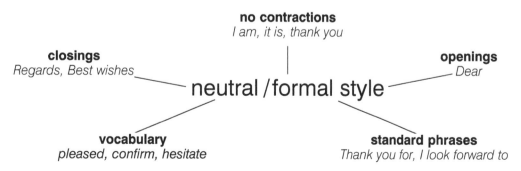

no contractions
I am, it is, thank you

closings
Regards, Best wishes

openings
Dear

neutral / formal style

vocabulary
pleased, confirm, hesitate

standard phrases
Thank you for, I look forward to

Formal letters

1 **Read the letter below and the tips on how to write formal letters.**

On headed paper, start the letter with the name and address of the person you are writing to.

Always date the letter.

Use a reference line to say what the subject of the letter is.

Always use an appropriate opening. (See opposite.)

If there has been previous contact, refer to it.

Always set the letter out in clear paragraphs.

Short forms, e.g. *we're* or *don't* are not normally used in formal letters.

Always use an appropriate closing. (See opposite.)

Sign the letter. Type your name and job title.

cc the names of anyone who will also receive a copy of the letter.

Taragon, Inc.

2722 NW 77th Street
Miami
Florida 33166
Tel: 001 305 277-3006
Fax: 001 305 277-3450
info@taragon-sales.com

Mr Edmundo Dias
Taragano do Brasil
Rua Emilio Goeldi 246
Lapa
05065 São Paulo

11 December 2011

Re: Trade Fair 14–18 February 2012

Dear Mr Dias

Further to your letter of 22 November, I am happy to say that we are now in a position to confirm our participation in the São Paulo Trade Fair on the above dates.

We would be very grateful if you could send us a plan of the exhibition hall and indicate which areas are still available and the respective prices.

We would like to participate for all four days of the fair and estimate that we would need a display area of approximately 100–120m^2. I will be able to confirm this information once I have received your plan and price schedule.

I would also be very grateful for any information on the expected visitor numbers and on your marketing campaign. Will you be marketing the fair in the US this year? This information would be invaluable in fixing our budget for the exhibition.

We are quite keen to move quickly on this and secure the best display area available. Therefore, I would very much appreciate a quick reply from you.

I look forward to hearing from you soon.

Yours sincerely

Phoebe Cornell
(Corporate Communications)

cc: Jefferson Taylor

2 Here are some useful phrases when writing letters.

Openings
Dear Sir / Madam
Dear Mr Evans
Dear Francesca

Closings
Yours faithfully
Yours sincerely
Kind / Best regards

Referring to previous contact
With reference to your letter of …
Further to our phone call of …
Thank you for your enquiry / email of …

Enclosures / attachments
Please find the enclosed / attached …
I enclose the …
I have attached a …

Requesting / Asking for information
I am writing to enquire about …
We would be very grateful if you could …
Would it be possible to …
Could you please …

Giving information
Please note that …
I would like to inform you that …
I trust you will find the following points of interest.

Checking information
Please let me know as soon as possible.
Could you please confirm …
I would be grateful if you could confirm …

Suggesting / recommending
May I suggest / propose …
We could / should …
It is suggested / proposed that …

Complaining
I would like to complain about the …
Unless …, we will be forced to …
I therefore urge you to …

Apologising
We apologise for …
We are sorry about the …
We apologise for any inconvenience.

Finishing a letter
If you have any further questions, please do not hesitate to contact us.
We look forward to seeing / meeting you on …
I look forward to hearing from you.

3 Read the following note from a colleague and write a suitable letter of reply.

Sam

We've got some problems with an order which arrived today from Yardley's. They sent only 200 small ladies' jeans rather than the 400 we ordered (cat no: JNW606m). Also, some of the men's T-shirts arrived damaged. The delivery company says it was bad packaging that allowed them to get wet. There are about twenty packets that are damaged (TSM40XL).

Could you please write to Yardley's and ask for the extra jeans and replacement T-shirts? This isn't the first time we've had problems so tell them (politely, of course) that if they don't improve we'll start to look for another supplier.

The contact who deals with our orders is Michelle Wilson. The address is Yardley Fashions, 86 Heathcoat Way, Colchester, Essex CM20 4GF.

Thanks.

Formal reports

1 Read the report below and the tips on how to write formal reports.

Always give the report a title.

Begin by stating the aims / purpose of the report in the *Introduction*.

In the *Findings* section, discuss the advantages / disadvantages of proposals.

Always set the report out in clear paragraphs.

Use linking words to connect ideas.

Do not use informal language or short forms e.g. *It's, don't*.

In the *Conclusion* say which idea is best and why.

Finish with a *Recommendation* or *Summary* section.

Use standard phrases where possible.

Finish with your name and date.

Report on sales staff training proposal

Introduction

The purpose of this report is to consider two proposed team-building activities for the sales staff and then recommend the most suitable.

Findings

Our research into suppliers of management team-building services found two possible solutions. The first, Executive Adventures Ltd, is a day of outdoor events involving both intellectual and physical challenges. The second one, Melville Management Training, is a two-day in-company seminar involving simulations.

The outdoor adventures would certainly be more appealing to staff and be seen as two days 'off work'. These would also be very motivating and staff would be grateful to the company for the opportunity to take part.

Although Melville are less exciting in comparison, they can design the seminar especially for our business needs. The simulations would use our own typical problems for workshops and therefore have a direct benefit for the participants. Staff, however, would see this as simply two days at work and not be grateful for the training.

Conclusion

Despite the direct benefits of Melville, it is felt that staff morale would be best served by the outdoor adventures.

Recommendation

It is recommended that suitable dates should be found to organise a two-day Executive Adventures course for all sales staff.

Jason Cozier
Human Relations Officer

October 2011

2 Which of these phrases can follow the verbs of recommending?

> a review of procedures   reviewing procedures   to review procedures
> that you review procedures   you to review procedures

we recommend	*a review of procedures*
we suggest	*a review of procedures*
we propose	*a review of procedures*
we advise	*a review of procedures*

3 Here are some useful phrases when writing reports.

Introduction
The aim / purpose of this report is to …
This report sets out to …
This report aims to …

Findings
It was found that …
Our research into … found …
… clearly shows that …
It became clear that …
… suggest that …

Contrasting ideas
However, …
Although ……
Despite / In spite of …
… while / whereas …

Linking cause and effect
because of / as a result of / due to …
This means …
Therefore, …
… leads to / results in …

Conclusion
It was concluded / decided / felt that …
No conclusions were reached regarding the …
In conclusion, / On balance, …

Recommendations
We would recommend / propose that …
It is recommended / suggested that …
We advise you to …

Summary
To summarise, …
In summary, …

Comparing ideas
Both / Neither …
Like / Unlike …
in comparison (with) …
… (not) as + adjective as …
more / less + adjective

Adding ideas
Furthermore, / Moreover, / In addition, …
… as well as …
also …

Preparing to write formal reports

1 Look at the instructions and the information below.

- You work for Freetime Foods. You have been asked to write a report summarising the company's performance in 2011.
- Look at the financial data and your handwritten notes below.
- Write a report of **120–140** words.

Freetime Foods: Financial Results 2011

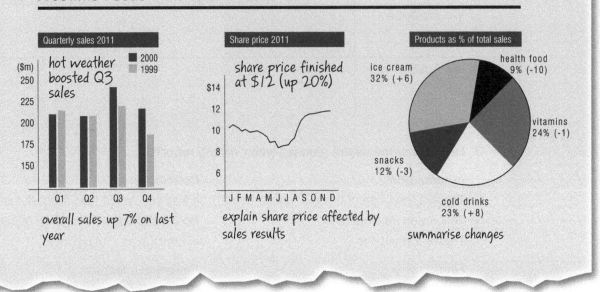

2 Now think about the following questions before starting to write and choose the most appropriate answers.

1 What kind of report is it?
    a) recommendation   **b)** summary   **c)** proposal

2 What sections will I need? (tick as appropriate)
    a) Introduction   **b)** Findings   **c)** Summary
    d) Conclusion   **e)** Proposal   **f)** Recommendation

3 Which phrases will be useful in the first section? (tick as appropriate)
    a) The aim of this report is to …   **b)** I'd like to talk about …
    c) The purpose of this report is to …   **d)** In this report I'm going to talk about …

4 How many paragraphs will I need in the main section?
    a) One – keep all the information together.
    b) Two – one for good points and one for bad points.
    c) Three – one for each graph and chart.
    d) Five – one for each handwritten note.

5 Which standard phrases will be useful in the final section? (tick as appropriate)
    a) It became clear that …
    b) On balance, …
    c) It was agreed that …
    d) To summarise, …
    e) We would recommend that …

3 Now make some detailed notes of what needs to go into the report. Use the linking words in the box to write full sentences.

> although   due to   however   despite   resulted in

1 sales down on last year to begin – sales boosted by hot weather in Q3

Although sales began down on last year, they were boosted by the hot weather in the third quarter.

2 slow start to the year – overall sales up 7% on last year

_____

_____

3 shares fell to $8 in June – poor sales figures

_____

_____

4 hot weather – sales nearly reached $250m in the third quarter

_____

_____

5 good growth in ice cream & cold drinks – sharp drop in health food sales

_____

_____

4 Look at the following report on Freetime Foods' financial results for 2011. How could the report be improved?

Overall, I think the company did quite well in 2011. But not every part of the company did well. The results were better at the end of the year than at the start. Overall, sales were up 7% on last year. The hot weather boosted sales in Q3, which was very good. The share price of the company finished at $12. This was 20% up on the start of the year, which was very good. The share price was affected by sales results. The products that did best were ice cream, which was up 6 per cent on last year and cold drinks, which were up 8% on last year. Health food did very badly. It was down 10 per cent on last year. This is a problem. Snacks and vitamins were almost the same as last year. Snacks fell 3% and vitamins by one per cent. I think the company did OK.

5 Now write your own 120–140 word report on Freetime Foods' financial performance using all the information and advice on these pages.

Answer key (Units 1–10)

Unit 1: Management

Grammar practice

1 2 do
3 do you report
4 doesn't she like
5 authorises

6 doesn't have
7 don't have
8 supervises

2 2 'm trying
3 is restructuring
4 isn't performing
5 are you scheduling

6 is taking
7 aren't going
8 're finding

3 2 need
3 want
4 is organising
5 believe
6 is negotiating

7 doesn't sound
8 make
9 authorises
10 think

4 2 does he?
3 will we?
4 don't they?

5 isn't she?
6 are we?

Vocabulary practice

1 2 chief executive (CEO)
3 brainstorming
4 counter-productive
5 decision-making
6 points of view

7 unanimous
8 casting vote
9 summary
10 minutes

2 2 negotiate a deal
3 authorise a payment
4 submit a report
5 control costs
6 cast a vote
7 reorganise the company structure
8 delegate a task

3 2 e
3 a
4 g
5 h

6 f
7 d
8 c

4 1 objectives
2 on the job
3 pie chart
4 consultant

5 schedule
6 team member
7 trainee
8 participant
9 goal

5 administer, administrator, administrative
assist, assistance
organisation, organisational
partner, partnership

representation
analyse, analyst, analytical
supervise, supervision, supervisory

2 representative
3 supervisory
4 analytical
5 administration
6 partnership
7 assist
8 organisational

Unit 2: Customers

Grammar practice

1 1 reorganised
2 did the clients arrive
3 Did you take
4 wasn't
5 got

6 took
7 didn't want
8 Did you secure
9 didn't finalise
10 didn't have

2 2 came
3 spoke
4 passed
5 did she say
6 gave
7 asked
8 've already done
9 asked
10 've already received

11 Did you find
12 didn't do
13 helped
14 has he been
15 got
16 have you done
17 haven't received
18 've brought

3 2 for
3 recently
4 already
5 yet

6 ever
7 ago
8 since

Vocabulary practice

1

E	V	S	S	Y	D	N	E	Y	Y	O	E
S	I	G	H	T	S	E	E	I	N	G	T
T	G	C	O	N	C	E	R	T	F	A	C
H	G	O	P	E	G	O	L	E	O	L	R
E	R	L	P	G	F	P	P	N	O	L	I
A	A	D	I	N	N	E	R	N	T	E	C
T	N	R	N	L	W	R	U	I	B	R	K
R	D	U	G	K	R	A	G	S	A	Y	E
E	P	G	F	O	O	T	B	A	L	L	T
S	R	B	T	E	N	N	Y	P	T	S	R
E	I	P	H	O	R	S	E	R	A	C	E
P	X	G	R	G	O	L	F	O	P	E	R

2 dinner, 3 rugby, 4 football, 5 opera, 6 theatre, 7 horse race, 8 concert, 9 shopping, 10 gallery, 11 tennis, 12 cricket, 13 golf, 14 grand prix

2

verb	noun	person
claim	claim	claimant
negotiate	negotiation	**negotiator**
consume	**consumption**	consumer
distribute	distribution	**distributor**
host	**host**	host

2 negotiate
3 host
4 distribution
5 claimants
6 consumption

3 meet: customers, objectives
win: customers, orders, contracts
establish: relationships, objectives
cancel: orders, contracts
manage: customers, relationships

4 2 colleagues
3 satisfaction
4 inconvenience
5 valued customer
6 substantial
7 after-sales service
8 value for money

5 See sample answer on page 76.

Unit 3: Commerce

Grammar practice

1 1 lands
2 'm picking
3 're sending
4 doesn't arrive
5 'm opening
6 'm seeing
7 are starting
8 are going

2 1 b
2 c
3 g
4 e
5 d
6 a
7 f

3 2 'll just get
3 'll get
4 are starting
5 Are you taking
6 'll be / 're going to be
7 won't fulfil
8 'll definitely need / 'm definitely going to need
9 will / 's going to lend
10 'll / are going to want
11 'm seeing / 'm going to see
12 'll see
13 won't / isn't going to be
14 'll need / 'm going to need

Vocabulary practice

1 PEOPLE
payee, creditor, adviser, cashier, banker

PAPERS
advice note, paying-in slip, counterfoil, statement

ACCOUNT MANAGEMENT
credit, deduct, transaction, interest, deposit, debit

2 2 g
3 i
4 f
5 h
6 a
7 j
8 c
9 e
10 d

3 2 a bank – interest on savings – an account holder
3 an importer – customs duty – the government
4 the government – tax relief – a tax payer
5 an account holder – bank charges – a bank
6 a company – a dividend – shareholders

4 2 payment
3 transaction
4 discount
5 cash
6 note
7 code
8 condition
9 cheque
10 duty

5 b – e – c – g – d – a – f

6 2 arrange haulage
3 fill in a delivery note
4 negotiate with the supplier
5 pay import duty
6 ship a consignment

Unit 4: Brands

Grammar practice

1 1 much
2 any
3 few
4 any
5 All
6 Both
7 little
8 a lot of
9 every
10 some

2 2 ~~little~~ / few
3 ~~the~~ / ø
4 ~~few~~ / little
5 ~~an~~ / the
6 ~~both~~ / each
7 ~~many~~ / much
8 ~~many~~ / any
9 ~~an~~ / some
10 ~~much~~ / many

3 2 a
3 the
4 a / the
5 Ø
6 Ø
7 an
8 A
9 Ø
10 Ø
11 a
12 a
13 the
14 an
15 Ø

Vocabulary practice

1 2 Dell – US – computers
3 BMW – German – cars
4 IKEA – Swedish – furniture
5 Benetton – Italian – clothes
6 Sony – Japanese – computer games
7 Nokia – Finnish – mobile phones
8 L'Oréal – French – cosmetics

2 1 price
2 performance
3 after-sales service

4 user-friendliness
5 image

3 2 power
3 admit
4 issue
5 conditions
6 customers

7 policy
8 insurance
9 companies
10 concerns

4 2 withheld funding
3 comply with policies
4 bring about change
5 run a business
6 stretched their brand
7 carry product lines
8 provide healthcare
9 cling to ideals
10 creating loyalty

5 2 brand loyalty
3 brand awareness
4 household name
5 pricing policy
6 loss-leader
7 premium

Unit 5: Facilities

Grammar practice

1 2 the farthest / furthest
3 the easiest
4 expensive as
5 the most important
6 most attractive

7 the best
8 the most expensive
9 the largest
10 more efficiently
11 better

2 2 exciting
3 networked
4 returning
5 Having finished
6 interesting

7 invested
8 newly-constructed
9 Having relocated
10 interested
11 invested

3 2 long-lasting
3 mass-produced
4 air-conditioned

5 fully-automated
6 long-running

Vocabulary practice

1 ▶ **Across**
1 premises
4 factory
5 contractor
8 investment
9 leasehold
10 assembly

▼ **Down**
1 plant
2 site
3 machinery
6 automate
7 upgrade

2 g – b – f – a – d – h – c – e – i

3 INFRASTRUCTURE
motorways, public transport, road access, waterways, airports

COST FACTORS
grants, renovation costs, running costs, rent

LABOUR MARKET
skills, availability of workers, employment law, local wage levels

4 INTRODUCTION
The purpose of this report is to ...
This report aims to ...
This report sets out to ...

CONCLUSION
It was decided that ...
It was felt that ...
No decision was reached regarding ...

RECOMMENDATION
It is suggested that ...
We would suggest that ...
It is proposed that ...

5 See sample answer on page 76.

Unit 6: Reporting

Grammar practice

1 1 steadily
2 sharp
3 slight
4 steady
5 dramatic
6 increasingly

7 extremely
8 slowly
9 slow
10 brief
11 sharply
12 suddenly

2 2 e
3 f
4 a
5 d

6 h
7 c
8 g

3 2 They wrote off $400,000 of bad debts which / that / Ø they couldn't recover.
3 Michael O'Leary is the CEO of Ryanair, which is a low-cost airline.
4 Nick Leeson was the trader whose dealings put Barings Bank out of business.
5 The figures didn't include tax, which makes a big difference.

Vocabulary practice

1 1 peak
2 shoot up
3 recover
4 reach a target
5 halve
6 collapse
7 remain steady
8 fluctuate

2

sharply	**steadily**	**slightly**
fluctuate	rise	fluctuate
rise	improve	rise
improve	fall	improve
fall		fall

3 2 to
3 by
4 of
5 at
6 by
7 at
8 in
9 in
10 in

4 2 d
3 a
4 f
5 g
6 h
7 c
8 e

5 2 i
3 e
4 g
5 f
6 h
7 d
8 c
9 a

6 See sample answer on page 77.

Unit 7: The workplace

Grammar practice

1 1 might
2 mustn't
3 May
4 should
5 'll
6 can
7 can
8 'll have

2 2 She might (others express permission)
3 I must (others express ability)
4 He's allowed to (others express possibility)
5 They don't have to (others express obligation)
6 Will I (others express permission or requests)
7 We will (others express suggestions)
8 I may (others express offers)

3 1 is based
2 happened
3 was witnessed
4 confirms
5 was asked
6 were delivered
7 were all stored
8 asked
9 was being lifted
10 lost
11 was called
12 realised
13 called
14 arrived
15 was taken

1 Vocabulary practice

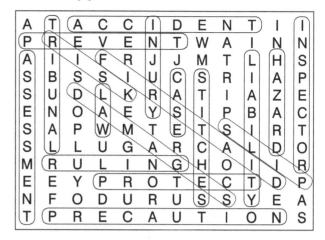

2 injury
3 prevent
4 first aid
5 risk
6 stitches
7 liability
8 slip
9 tribunal
10 case
11 assessment
12 damages
13 law
14 inspector
15 hazard
16 precaution
17 protect
18 ruling

2 2 maternity leave
3 shop steward
4 wage packet
5 disciplinary procedure
6 sickness benefit
7 hourly rate
8 social security

3 2 disciplinary
3 time off
4 absent
5 time-keeping
6 sue
7 rights
8 unfair dismissal
9 notify
10 ultimatum

4 2 e
3 g
4 a
5 f
6 c
7 d

5 2 absence
3 fraudulent
4 liability
5 exempt
6 suspended

Unit 8: Business travel

Grammar practice

1 1 ... what gate number it is?
2 ... where the check-in desk is?
3 ... if/whether you have any foreign currency?
4 ... if/whether you got any frequent-flyer miles?
5 ... when you left?
6 ... if/whether they've reimbursed your expenses?
7 ... why there is a delay?
8 ... how this seat reclines?

2 2 ... complained about waiting for over three hours.
3 ... suggested trying to get an upgrade.
4 ... reminded me to take my passport.
5 ... refused to book the hotel room for me.
6 ... offered to phone the hotel and book a room.
7 ... warned me not to go out on my own at night.
8 ... recommended staying at the Park Plaza Hotel.
9 ... denied changing any information on his ...
10 ... invited us to stay with them for a weekend.

3 1 complain (others followed by an infinitive)
2 refuse (others followed by *that*)
3 explain (others followed by an infinitive)
4 remind (others followed by a gerund)

Vocabulary practice

1 2 connecting flight
3 onboard entertainment
4 departure lounge
5 frequent flyer
6 boarding gate
7 foreign currency
8 excess baggage

2 1 refreshments
2 online
3 proof
4 check-in
5 allocation
6 cancellation
7 transferred
8 refunds

3 1 claim
2 authorise
3 check-in
4 entertainment
5 delegate
6 package

4 1 plus, equals / comes to
2 deduct
3 multiply
4 add
5 divide
6 times
7 Add
8 minus

5 2 scan receipts
3 reimburse expenses
4 implementing / system
5 processing claims
6 log in to / account

6 See sample answer on page 77.

Unit 9: People

Grammar practice

1 1 b   3 c   5 h   7 e
2 d   4 a   6 f   8 g

2 1 to find
2 to get
3 to be
4 to bring
5 filling
6 not being
7 working / to work
8 to sound
9 manage
10 to meet
11 to get
12 not to have
13 to get
14 asking
15 to get
16 working
17 Meeting
18 travelling
19 visiting
20 working

Vocabulary practice

1 REMUNERATION
award, take-home pay, salary scale, benefits, wage

DEVELOPMENT
promotion, upgrade, potential, prospects

PERFORMANCE
results, time management, targets, objectives, record

2

verb	noun
criticise	criticism
notify	**notification**
assign	**assignment**
approve	approval
develop	**development**
permit	**permission**
remunerate	remuneration
evaluate	**evaluation**

2 notification
3 remuneration
4 evaluate
5 development
6 criticism
7 permit
8 approve
9 assign

3 1 b   5 g
2 f   6 h
3 e   7 d
4 a   8 c

4 1 retirement
2 testimonial
3 council
4 aptitude
5 shift
6 vacation
7 redundancy
8 quantity

5 1 rank
2 temp
3 basic wage
4 references
5 headhunt
6 advertise
7 shortlist

Unit 10: Marketing

Grammar practice

1 1 don't go
2 will increase
3 switch
4 won't know
5 'll / 're going to rethink
6 doesn't win
7 don't / can't find
8 sells

2 2 We'd give free samples if they didn't cost so much money.
3 Our website would be more attractive if we had a trained graphic designer.
4 If we'd gone to the trade fair, we'd have seen our competitor's new products.
5 We could do a mailshot if our mailing list were larger.
6 The product would have sold better if it hadn't had the bad publicity in the newspapers.
7 More customers would subscribe to the website if they'd heard about it.

8 If the TV advert hadn't been so popular, the product wouldn't have sold so well.
9 If we want the product to sell well in Germany, we'll have to change the name.
10 We wouldn't have had the quality problems if we'd delayed the launch by six weeks.

3 1 will / is going to sell, target, launch
2 wouldn't have been, hadn't made
3 wouldn't target, were, 'd go
4 wouldn't have been, 'd continued
5 'd / could boost, redesigned, would be
6 'll / can, open

Vocabulary practice

1 DISTRIBUTION
subscription, outlets, chain stores, franchise, direct selling

MARKET TRENDS
flood, dominate, saturate, boom, break into

PROMOTION
free sample, exhibition, sponsorship, media, word of mouth, TV adverts

2 1 b   6 i
2 f   7 d
3 g   8 e
4 h   9 c
5 a

3 1 lifestyle   4 slogan
2 saturate   5 prospectus
3 billboard   6 jingle

4 | verb | noun |
|---|---|
| publicise | **publicity** |
| **launch** | launch |
| license | **licence** |
| **feed back** | feedback |
| differentiate | **differentiation** |
| position | **positioning** (as a marketing term) |
| **campaign** | campaign |

2 differentiate   6 feedback
3 publicity   7 license
4 campaign   8 launch
5 position

5 1 report   5 logo
2 discounted   6 retailer
3 performance   7 franchise
4 packaging   8 dominate

6 See sample answer on page 78.

Writing

Letters and emails

1 Informal style:
Opening: *Hi Monica*
Contractions: *That's, I'm*
Vocabulary: *great, can, really, getting*
Closing: *Thanks & regards*

2 2 f   4 a   6 g   8 c
3 e   5 h   7 d

3 See sample answer on page 78.

Formal letters

3 See sample answer on page 79.

Formal reports

2 we recommend: a review of, reviewing, that you review, you to review
we suggest: a review, reviewing, that you review
we propose: a review of, reviewing, to review
we advise: a review of, you to review

Preparing to write formal reports

2 1 b   2 a, b, c   3 a, c   4 c   5 b, d

3 2 Despite a slow start, overall sales were up 7% on last year.
3 Shares fell to $8 in June due to poor sales figures.
4 Hot weather resulted in sales reaching nearly $250m in the third quarter.
5 There was good growth in ice cream and soft drinks. However, there was a sharp drop in health food sales.

4 Candidate's mistakes:
• no use of structure or paragraphs
• no use of standard phrases and linking words
• use of inappropriate informal vocabulary
• copying of text from question material

5 See sample answer on page 79.

Review units

Review 1 (Units 1–5) Grammar

1
1. 's just finishing
2. are you shipping
3. 're using
4. don't use
5. have
6. 're trying
7. seem
8. 're giving
9. are you sending
10. does the ship leave / is the ship leaving
11. leaves
12. think
13. 're loading
14. don't want
15. 's calling

2
1. much
2. few
3. All
4. some
5. a lot of
6. all
7. little
8. some
9. many
10. any

3
1. 've already sent
2. 've invited
3. haven't responded
4. spoke
5. said
6. planned
7. 's done
8. 's even asked
9. 's known
10. arranged
11. didn't mention
12. spoke
13. found
14. was
15. told

4
1. ago
2. yet
3. OK
4. OK
5. for
6. OK
7. for
8. OK
9. never
10. OK

5
1. 'll be / 'm going to be
2. 'll have / 're going to have
3. 'll type / 's going to type
4. are arriving
5. 're flying
6. lands / 's landing
7. is picking
8. might / may want
9. won't get
10. 're going / 'll go
11. are both coming
12. 're going
13. Will you have / Are you going to have
14. 'll be / 're going to be
15. 're meeting
16. 'll take / 'm going to take

6
1. better
2. the best
3. tougher than
4. more careful
5. as happy
6. more efficiently than
7. the highest
8. as good as
9. less experienced
10. earlier

7
1. interested
2. targeted
3. newly-developed
4. fast-growing
5. Having received
6. short-sighted
7. well-invested
8. Having done
9. mass-marketing
10. interesting

8
1. the
2. the
3. Ø
4. Ø
5. the
6. the
7. Ø
8. an
9. Ø / the
10. the
11. the
12. a
13. Ø
14. a
15. the

Review 1 (Units 1–5) Vocabulary

1. b) flow chart
2. c) loan
3. c) counterfeit
4. a) warranty
5. a) authorise
6. c) backlog
7. b) loss-leader
8. c) interest
9. b) location
10. a) unanimous
11. a) satisfaction
12. b) AOB
13. c) claimant
14. c) structure
15. a) diversify
16. b) upgrading
17. c) advantage
18. a) distribution
19. b) allocate
20. c) receivers
21. c) awareness
22. c) tender
23. a) deposit
24. b) establishing
25. b) outstanding
26. c) ethical
27. c) infrastructure
28. a) cost-effective
29. b) track record
30. a) slogans
31. c) satisfy
32. b) supervision
33. a) tariff
34. a) haulage
35. c) inflation
36. c) discontinued
37. b) expenses
38. a) point
39. b) patent
40. c) substantial
41. b) start-up
42. c) line manager
43. b) delegates
44. c) assistant
45. c) stretched
46. a) comply with
47. c) delivery
48. b) return
49. a) policy
50. b) outlets

Review 2 (Units 6–10) Grammar

1
1 The design was patented in 2008.
2 The market has been dominated by a local ...
3 A new product is being launched in May.
4 The goods are produced under a licensing ...
5 The campaign wasn't organised early enough.
6 The market is being saturated by cheap ...
7 Our margins are going to be reduced by 6%.
8 How was the product positioned?
9 The product needs to be differentiated enough ...
10 How has the new product been marketed?
11 Over 2,000 questionnaires were filled in ...
12 A new jingle has been written for the TV ...
13 The product should have been been promoted ...
14 The product wasn't launched until it was ...
15 They're given to customers for free.

2
1	Could	9	'll see
2	might	10	can
3	have	11	'll
4	won't	12	Could
5	can	13	can
6	don't have to	14	won't
7	'm going to	15	can
8	'll mention		

3
2	who	7	who /that
3	which	8	which /that
4	Whose	9	which /that
5	Who	10	Ø /which /that
6	which /that		

4
1	sharply	6	slow
2	significant	7	sharply
3	slight	8	real
4	increasingly	9	urgent
5	dramatically	10	exact

5
2 ... when the flight for Wellington is leaving?
3 ... where I have to check in for the Paris flight?
4 ... where check-in zone D is?
5 ... how long before the flight I have to check in?
6 ... if /whether you packed your own luggage?
7 ... how many suitcases you'd like to check in?
8 ... if /whether anyone has given you anything to take on board?
9 ... where I can buy a newspaper?
10 ... whether /if you have a UK driving licence?

6
2 ... us not to take on any new workers.
3 ... to see some profit by the end of the year.
4 ... (that) Peter was getting married.
5 ... to cut prices.
6 ... me not to say anything about the sales figures.
7 ... about never getting enough information.
8 ... to send me the figures this /that week.
9 ... (that) market conditions had been very tough.
10 ... me not to announce the figures until after the shareholders' meeting.

7
1	would have done	9	hold on
2	hadn't performed	10	make
3	look	11	would have been
4	look	12	'd bought
5	could have been	13	were
6	hadn't invested	14	'd look
7	wouldn't sell	15	say
8	were		

8
1	speaking	9	not having
2	to send	10	cleaning
3	going	11	talking
4	to write	12	to say
5	to see	13	looking
6	to say	14	seeing
7	to come	15	to solve
8	seeing		

Review 2 (Units 6–10) Vocabulary

1	b) saturated	26	a) hazard
2	b) reimbursed	27	b) loss-leader
3	c) wage	28	b) maternity
4	a) description	29	c) slipped
5	a) connecting	30	b) fluctuations
6	a) slump	31	a) remuneration
7	c) appointment	32	b) withdraw
8	a) jingle	33	c) schedule
9	c) cancelled	34	c) objective
10	a) white-collar	35	a) outlets
11	c) attorney	36	b) headhunter
12	c) receipts	37	a) subscriptions
13	a) references	38	b) shortage
14	a) mailshot	39	a) gate
15	a) Risk	40	c) potential
16	a) deals with	41	c) appraise
17	b) appraisal	42	c) publicity
18	b) point-of-sale	43	b) trade union
19	b) recession	44	b) process
20	a) differentiate	45	b) black
21	c) court	46	a) turnover
22	a) plaintiff	47	a) excess baggage
23	c) campaign	48	c) boom
24	c) strike	49	b) bankruptcy
25	c) surplus	50	b) timekeeping

Sample formal letter: Unit 2, Exercise 5

Re: Order no. 2001036MT

Dear Mr Carson

Thank you for your letter of 2 July regarding our order. We are sorry to hear about your difficulties and hope they have all been solved. We are happy to proceed with the order and would be grateful if you could send confirmation of the new delivery date.

We would also like to know whether it is possible to add a further two motors (catalogue no. 2203E) to the order.

We would like to take advantage of your offer concerning the discounted extended warranty. Could you please enclose the agreement with the delivery?

Could you please amend the invoice in accordance with these changes and send it to us?

I look forward to hearing from you soon.

Yours sincerely

Sample report: Unit 5, Exercise 5

Report on location of new assembly plant

Introduction

The purpose of this report is to assess the suitability of locating the new assembly plant in Hamburg, north Germany, and recommend a suitable site.

Findings

Hamburg has excellent transport links by sea, road, rail and air. It is one of Europe's busiest ports, Germany's two main motorways pass through the city and it has a fast-growing international airport. It is also a gateway to Scandinavia and central Europe with a fast rail link to Berlin.

The region has an educated and skilled workforce with a strong engineering tradition. It will be possible to source many components locally.

Recommendation

It is suggested that the fast-developing business park north west of the city would be an ideal site because it is next to the motorway and 10 minutes from both the harbour and rail terminal. We recommend that the site should be studied in more detail immediately.

Sample report: Unit 6, Exercise 6

Report on Stanton, Inc. 2011

Introduction

This report aims to assess the Stanton, Inc. 2011 balance sheet and make a recommendation regarding whether we should invest in Stanton shares.

Findings

Stanton seems to have had difficulties in selling its products in 2011. This could have been due to difficult trading conditions or ageing and unpopular products. Furthermore, the increase in money owed by debtors suggests that customers are also having difficulties.

Stanton has also increased its own debt to the banks yet little of this has been invested in new plant and machinery for the future.

Conclusion

Stanton has had a difficult year and now has surplus stock, cash flow problems and substantially increased debt.

Recommendation

It is recommended that we do not invest in Stanton at the present but review the situation in six months' time.

Sample formal letter: Unit 8, Exercise 6

Re: Your visit 24–26 May

Dear Mrs Gudjohnson

Thank you for your letter of 24 April. We are delighted that you are able to make the trip and have prepared the following itinerary for your visit.

Thursday 24 May

10.40   Arrive Frankfurt airport. We will arrange for a taxi to meet you and bring you straight to the company.

11.30   Tour of the company.

12.30   Lunch with Mirijana Kurtz.

14.00   Visit SKA GmbH in Wiesbaden. (Return to hotel by 17.00.)

20.00   Dinner with Pierre Bonner.

Friday 25 May

09.00   Visit Kahn & Sohn, a supplier.

13.00   Lunch in Frankfurt.

14.30   Meeting with MD Michael Thomas and Sales Director Suzanna Köpke. (To finish at about 17.00.)

We have booked your return flight for Saturday morning at 08.40. You will need to confirm this flight 24 hours in advance. If you have any questions, please do not hesitate to contact us.

We look forward to seeing you soon.

Sample report: Unit 10, Exercise 6

Report on Dayton sales performance 2011

Introduction

This report summarises our 2011 sales performance in terms of market share, sales compared to competitors and regional results.

Findings

Although we are still the leader with 31% market share, the figure is down 6% on last year. Most of this was lost to our fastest-growing competitor, Allbright, whose new products and investment in advertising increased sales by 8%.

Despite growing 5% to $38.5m, sales were disappointing in a year when the overall market grew by a substantial 25%.

Sales in Europe and Asia slumped by 25% and 40% due to our competitors producing locally and selling more cheaply through a local sales force.

Recommendation

After such poor results, it is recommended that urgent action is taken to develop new products as soon as possible. The company should also look at setting up local production in Europe and Asia.

Sample email: Writing: Letters and emails, Exercise 3

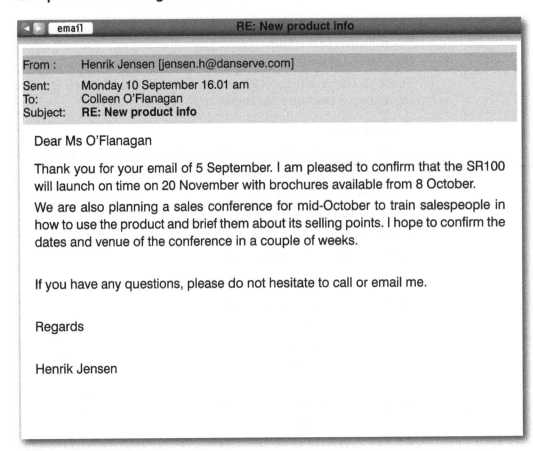

◄ ► email	RE: New product info

From :	Henrik Jensen [jensen.h@danserve.com]
Sent:	Monday 10 September 16.01 am
To:	Colleen O'Flanagan
Subject:	**RE: New product info**

Dear Ms O'Flanagan

Thank you for your email of 5 September. I am pleased to confirm that the SR100 will launch on time on 20 November with brochures available from 8 October.

We are also planning a sales conference for mid-October to train salespeople in how to use the product and brief them about its selling points. I hope to confirm the dates and venue of the conference in a couple of weeks.

If you have any questions, please do not hesitate to call or email me.

Regards

Henrik Jensen

Sample formal letter: Writing: Formal letters, Exercise 3

Re: Order no. 003456

Dear Ms Wilson

Thank you for the order which we received today. Unfortunately, there are problems with the order that I would like to bring to your attention.

Firstly, the quantity of small ladies jeans (cat no. JNW606M) is incorrect. We ordered 400 units but received only 200 units. Could you please send the remaining part of the order as soon as possible.

Secondly, about 20 packets of the men's T-shirts (cat no. TSM40XL) arrived damaged. The delivery company says bad packaging allowed them to get wet. We therefore ask you to replace these items.

We have had problems with several deliveries from you recently. I am sure you understand that it is essential for our business that orders arrive on time, correctly and in good condition. If you cannot guarantee this, then I am afraid we will have to consider alternative suppliers.

I look forward to hearing from you soon.

Sample report: Writing: Preparing to write formal reports, Exercise 5

Report on Freetime Foods' performance 2011

Introduction
The purpose of this report is to summarise our 2011 results in terms of turnover, share price and sales of product categories.

Findings
Despite a slow start, turnover was up 7% on last year. This was mainly due to the hot weather in July and August.
Shares fell steadily in the first half of the year due to poor sales results, falling from $10 to $8. However, they finished 20% up at the end of the year as news of strong Q3 sales reached investors.
There was good growth in ice cream and soft drinks. However, there was a sharp drop in health food sales.

Summary
Despite a slow start, the company finished the year with 7% sales growth, a substantially higher market value and strong growth in ice cream and soft drinks. The only disappointment was a 10% fall in health food sales.